PLANES

X

PUSHING THE ENVELOPE OF FLIGHT

MBI Publishing Company

DEDICATION

This reference is dedicated to the memory of the far too many aeronauts and astronauts who have lost their lives while making new—and sometimes old—aircraft and spacecraft as flight-worthy and safe as possible for their future users.

First published in 2003 by MBI Publishing Company, Galtier Plaza, Suite 200, 380 Jackson Street, St. Paul, MN 55101-3885 USA

MBI Publishing Company titles are also available at discounts in bulk quantity for industrial or sales-promotional use. For details write to S pecial Sales Manager at Motorbooks International Wholesalers & Distributors, Galtier Plaza, Suite 200, 380 Jackson Street, St. Paul, MN 55101-3885 USA

Library of Congress Cataoging-in-Publication Data

Pace, Steve.
    X-Planes : America's research aricraft / by Steve Pace
        p. cm.
    Included bibliography reference and index.
    ISBN 0-7603-1584-1 (pbk. : alk. paper)
    1. Reasrch aircraft--United States--History. I. Title.

TL567.R47P3297 2003
629.133'0973--dc21

Front cover: The one-of-a-kind *Bird of Prey* was produced by the Boeing Phantom Works and flight tested from fall 1996 through the year 1999. With its relatively new type of dorsal engine air inlet situated just aft of its canopy (very few aircraft have used this type of engine air inlet system), a single 3,190lb thrust class Pratt & Whitney JT15D-5C turbofan engine propelled it to its operational speed of 300mph and 20,000ft maximum operating altitude. *Boeing*

Back cover: *([BC-1])* Artist concept of operational Boeing A-45A "Shrike," based upon the X-45A. *Boeing ([BC-2])* Artist concept of operational Northrop Grumman A-47A Pegasus based upon the X-47A but with wings. *Northrop Grumman ([BC-3])* Boeing X-50A Dragonfly. *Boeing*

On the frontispiece: One of the three NASA-owned Lockheed SR-71 Blackbird aircraft; it has two single-seat SR-71As and a two-seat SR-71B. A single-seat SR-71A is shown. *NASA*

On the title page: The second of two North American XB-70A Valkyrie triplesonic research aircraft poses high in the sky somewhere near Edwards AFB in early 1966. The last flight of an XB-70A came on 4 February 1969 – nearly 35 years ago, yet it remains to be the biggest and heaviest airplane to have ever exceeded three-times-the-speed-of-sound or 2,000mph. *AFFTC/HO*

Edited by Steve Gansen and Heather Oakley
Designed by Stephanie Michaud

Printed in Hong Kong

Table of Contents

FOREWORD

IN APRIL 1942, a strange flurry of activity began on a remote area of Muroc Army Air Field. Men, trucks, and tents suddenly appeared on the barren northwestern shore of Muroc Dry Lake, six miles north of the bustling training base, and in a very short time the wooden skeletons of two buildings began to rise above the sand and greasewood. Within a month, a portable army Unicon hangar, a wooden barracks building, and a wooden water tower were in place, and the Army Air Forces' new Materiel Center Flight Test Site was ready for business.

The cause of all this activity became apparent on 19 September, when several heavily guarded boxcars were delivered to a railway siding nearby. The mysterious contents were swiftly transported to the new settlement. A few days later America's first jet plane, the XP-59A Airacomet, stood assembled and ready for testing, far from the curious eyes of friend or foe.

The Army Air Forces could not have chosen a better site for a secret aviation test project. The dry lake (later called Rogers Dry Lake), some 7 miles wide and 12 miles long, was easily the world's largest natural landing field, and its immense clay surface was hard enough to support the weight of any aircraft ever planned. Even better, the flying weather was superb, averaging some 360 days each year. And the western Mojave Desert was remote from population centers and sparsely settled, so that new and secret airplane types could be flight tested discreetly as well as safely.

Actually, the lakebed had been used to flight test aircraft long before the XP-59 had appeared. The first project of which there is a record was a two-seat scout biplane that the California Aeroplane & Motor Company flew in August 1917. Then, on 26 October 1929, Jack Northrop flew the first of his long series of experimental flying wings from Muroc's natural runway. The first flight of an experimental Curtiss canard fighters, the CW-24B (later, after being developed, the XP-55 Ascender) took to the air just five days before the Japanese attack on Pearl Harbor. In between these flights, a series of civilian individuals and companies—Waterman, McClatchie, and the Loughead (Lockheed) brothers—tested their newest creations here. In October 1941, the commander of the Army Air Corps, General "Hap" Arnold, chose the north end of the lake for testing of the army's "special weapons." Soon a series of unmanned glide bombs, drone aircraft, and generally strange contraptions began appeared in the local skies. The tradition of experimental flight work in the area had been well established by the time the Flight Test Site got under way.

Meanwhile, the Army Air Corps already had been here for several years, just a few miles south toward the middle of the dry lakebed. In 1933, "Hap" Arnold, then a lieutenant colonel commanding March Field down in Riverside, had decided that he needed to find a safe spot way out in the Mojave Desert where he could set up a range for bombing and gunnery practice. It was not long before his troops scratched a few aerial targets out of the dry soil along the eastern shore, not far from the desolate little hamlet of Muroc. Soon, squadrons of P-12s, P-26s, B-10s, and Keystone bombers began to cycle in and out of the March Field Bombing and Gunnery Range for training. As the war clouds began to thicken in 1939 and 1940, these activities stepped up dramatically. A permanent runway and several hangars were constructed across the lake at a place now known as South Base, and the expanded installation was renamed the Muroc Bombing and Gunnery Range. World War II brought pilots of B-24 and P-38 squadrons here for their final unit training before they went overseas. The range was renamed Muroc Army Air Base in July 1942, and 16 months later it became Muroc Army Air Field. By whatever name, it remained part of the Fourth Air Force, unlike the flight test site, which belonged to the army's Materiel Command.

Meanwhile, the flight test site to the north, renamed the Materiel Command Flight Test Base in 1942, remained administratively separate from its larger neighbor. Peacetime made it possible to consolidate these two bases, which were used for flight test evaluation, into one. The wide-open airspace and dependable flying weather at the combined site couldn't be better, and the location was close to the large aviation companies that had grown up along the West Coast during the war. After the consolidation, Captain "Chuck" Yeager took the first of the X-planes on the world's first supersonic flight on 14 October 1947.

Over the next two years, Colonel (soon to be Brigadier General) Albert Boyd, commander of the Flight Test Division at Wright Field, moved the division's test facility to Muroc, well away from the crowded skies of Dayton, Ohio. In September 1949, he arrived to take command of Muroc Air Force Base. Four months later, the base was renamed Edwards Air Force Base in honor of Captain Glen W. Edwards, who had died not long before in the crash of the YB-49 Flying Wing bomber.

The Air Force Flight Test Center (AFFTC) was established at Edwards on 25 June 1951, and the rest, as they say, is history. Fifty-five years later, the center's facilities have developed enormously in number and sophistication, and the base has matured into the world's premier flight test facility. More than 150 aircraft types have had their first flights at Edwards, and the center's highly trained personnel have done much to put the United States at the forefront of the world's aviation development.

—Raymond L. Puffer, Ph.D., Historian
Air Force Flight Test Center History Office
Edwards Air Force Base, California
2 October 2003

PREFACE

THIS REFERENCE DISCUSSES a relatively large number of significant American experimental airplanes, or X-planes, that were and continue to be built and flown in an ongoing effort to advance the way we fly. To safely fly at faster and faster speeds, to higher and higher altitudes, and for longer and longer distances than the Wright brothers, Orville and Wilbur, first did on 17 December 1903 in America's first X-plane, the 1903 Wright Flyer. On its first flight, that aircraft flew about 12 miles per hour at an altitude of some 10 feet for a distance of around 120 feet. By the end of that most important day in aviation history, the Wright brothers had extended the speed, altitude, time, and distance of their flyer to approximately 31 miles per hour, 30 feet, and 850 feet, with a duration of 59 seconds. Those four test flights on that historic day by America's first test pilot, Orville Wright, had at last introduced mankind to flight in something other than unpowered gliders and hot-air balloons.

The 1903 Wright Flyer was the world's first manned heavier-than-air air vehicle to be flown under self-powered, sustained, and controlled flight. Three days earlier, on 14 December 1903, Wilbur Wright had flown the airplane 105 feet in 3.5 seconds. However, since it crashed shortly after liftoff, that flight was not considered to be controlled or sustained.

There are literally hundreds of American X-planes that have been built and flown in the United States throughout the last century. And what a century it has been! It has been an event-filled 100 years, which began with the dawn of flight and later included manned landings on the Moon and even unmanned flight.

The many different types of aircraft that have been created over the last 100 years stagger the mind. These include piston-powered and propeller-driven airplanes, rotary-winged airplanes (gyrocopters and helicopters), turbojet-powered airplanes, and rocket-powered airplanes.

While this treatise cannot include each and every experimental aircraft due to space limitations, it does describe a fairly large number of the most significant ones. An eclectic array of manned and unmanned air vehicles are covered. The reader will quickly note that not all of the American X-planes in this reference carry the

X prefix. However, the aircraft herein all fall under the *experimental, prototype (Y)* and/or *dedicated research* categories.

On 17 December 2003 we will have reached the 100th anniversary of the pilot-controlled and self-propelled airplane flight. This most significant milestone already has been and will continue to be touted throughout this year—and rightly so, for taking flight was truly one of mankind's biggest dreams and one its greatest accomplishments.

— Steve Pace
24 July 2003

ACKNOWLEDGMENTS

I wish to thank the following: Mike "Dark Side" Beakley; Genesis Real Estate; Retired Colonel Joseph F. "Joe" Cotton (U.S. Air Force); Kathleen M. Cook, Naval Aircraft Programs Communications, The Boeing Company; Retired Lieutenant General Laurence C. "Bill" Craigie (U.S. Air Force); Retired Lieutenant Colonel Fitzhugh L. "Fitz" Fulton Jr. (U.S. Air Force, NASA); Dennis R. Jenkins; Clarence L. "Kelly" Johnson; Denny Lombard, Lockheed Martin Skunk Works; Stan Piet, Glenn L. Martin Aviation Museum; Lieutenant General David J. "Marshall" McCloud; Dr. Raymond L. Puffer, U.S. Air Force historian at Air Force Flight Test Center at Edwards Air Force Base, California; Erik Simonsen, manager of communications, Air Force Systems, The Boeing Company.

chapter one

OUT OF THE STONE AGE

IN MANY RESPECTS, the numerous piston-powered and propeller-driven aircraft built and flown prior to the jet- and rocket-powered aircraft eras were developed in aviation's "stone age." Nevertheless, without those early experimental aircraft, none of the later, more technologically sophisticated aircraft ever would have emerged. And a number of significant "stone age" aircraft carried the prefix 'X' as an experimental designation, including such military notables as the Boeing XB-17 Flying Fortress and XB-29 Superfortress, Consolidated XB-24 Liberator and XB-36 Peacemaker, Douglas XB-19, Grumman XF6F Hellcat and XF7F Tigercat, Lockheed XP-38 Lightning, Martin XB-26 Marauder, McDonnell XP-69, North American XP-51 Mustang and XP-82 Twin Mustang, Northrop XP-56 Black Bullet and XP-61 Black Widow, Republic XP-47 Thunderbolt, and so on.

But of course, a large number of other very important civilian air vehicles never held the 'X' that was used for experimental classification. Some of these include the Boeing B-247 airliner and B-314 flying boat, Douglas DC-3 and DC-7 airliners, Fokker Trimotor airliner, and the like.

None of the aforementioned aircraft could have earned their way in life without the many sometimes frustrating years of learn-as-you-go achievements by some very clever aeronautical and propulsion engineers and the relatively small number of extraordinary test pilots. They worked together to evolve the way we fly, from aircraft made of wood and fabric to aircraft made of metal alloys and composite materials.

They also put these aircraft through extensive flight test evaluations before the aircraft could be used by the military establishment or the public in general. While some aircraft were and are flight-tested near their place of manufacture, many others have to be tested at far-away places that are specifically designated for such evaluations. Some of these sites include the following:

U.S. Air Force Flight Test Center at Edwards Air Force Base in California.

The Flight Test Center continues to host a vast array of significant aircraft, manned and unmanned. Located on the western edge of the Mojave Desert, Edwards Air Force Base (AFB) is about 100 miles northeast of Los Angeles. It encompasses 301,000 acres and is situated around Rogers Dry Lake, a natural 44-square-mile *playa* (a flat area at the bottom of a desert basin, sometimes temporarily covered with shallow water).

Since the early 1940s, Edwards AFB has been the epicenter for many revolutions in flight, for it has played host to many of the U.S. armed forces' and NASA's most significant aircraft. Just a few of these include the Bell XP-59A Airacomet, America's first jet-powered airplane; the Bell X-1, the world's first supersonic airplane; the Douglas D-558-2 Skyrocket, the world's first doublesonic airplane; the North American F-100 Super Sabre, America's first operational supersonic fighter; and the Lockheed F-104 Starfighter, the world's first operational doublesonic fighter. Other important aircraft tested at Edwards AFB include the General Dynamics (Convair) B-58 Hustler, the world's first operational doublesonic bomber; the North American X-15, the world's first trisonic and hypersonic (Mach 4, 5 and 6) aircraft; the North American XB-70A Valkyrie, still the largest and heaviest air vehicle to ever exceed 2,000 miles per hour (Mach 3); and last but not least, the fleet of space shuttles, which remain the only operational air vehicles to take off as a rocket and land as an airplane.

Naval Air Station Patuxent River, Maryland

Naval Air Station (NAS) Patuxent River (Pax River) in Maryland is to the U.S. Navy what Edwards AFB is to the U.S. Air Force: a premier flight test center. Since its official commissioning on 1 April 1943, NAS Patuxent River has served as the U.S. Navy's chief aircraft development and test facility.

Four months after the commissioning, flight test, radio test, aircraft armament, and aircraft experimental and development squadrons were established. The station had established service test, electronics test, flight test, and tactical test divisions by the beginning of 1945.

At the end of 1945, with the hardships of World War II quickly becoming memories, the navy was looking forward to the Jet Age, when it too would be able to field fleets of jet-powered aircraft. To get its feet wet in the Jet Age, the navy first acquired a Bell YP-59A Airacomet.

Some of Pax River's first notable X-Planes included the piston-powered and propeller-driven Chance Vought XF4U-1 Corsair, the Douglas XBT2D-1 Skyraider, the Grumman XF6F-3 Hellcat, the XF7F-1 Tigercat, and the XF8F-1 Bearcat.

Since April 1943, NAS Pax River has continued to evaluate U.S. Navy and Marine Corps experimental and prototype aircraft on a daily basis. Two of the most recent aircraft evaluated are the single-seat Boeing F/A-18E and the tandem-seat F/A-18F Super Hornet twosome. Both have just recently entered into squadron service.

Area 51

The so-called Area 51, a highly restricted area within the boundaries of Nellis Air Force Base in southern Nevada where the CIA, U.S. Air Force, and other government entities test their top-secret aircraft, also is known as Dreamland, Groom Lake, and the Ranch.

Clarence L. "Kelly" Johnson, famous for his many Lockheed Skunk Works' designs such as the A-12, D-21, M-21, SR-71, TR-1, U-2, and YF-12, once sent one of his favorite test pilots, Anthony W. "Tony" LeVier, on a quest to find a suitable test sight for the U-2. LeVier found Groom Lake, a giant dry lake, which Johnson agreed was satisfactory for his needs. Since it mainly would be Kelly Johnson's test site, it was subsequently nicknamed "the Ranch," actually meaning Kelly's Ranch. At the time, in early 1954, Groom Lake was located in what was designated Restricted Area 51 (or R-51) of Nellis Air Force Base. Thus, to many government workers at the facility, it simply became known as Area 51.

The first known aircraft flight test program at Groom Lake was the testing of the then-highly classified, CIA-backed Lockheed U-2 spy

plane. Tony LeVier was chief engineering test pilot, and on 4 August 1955, he made the successful official first flight in the program. (The first U-2 airplane, known only as *Angel 1*, had made an accidental first flight on 29 July 1955 during a high-speed taxi test.)

Following the U-2 evaluation program came the Lockheed A-12 flight test program under CIA project Oxcart. The first official flight of A-12 No. 1, with Lockheed Skunk Works test pilot Louis W. "Lou" Schalk Jr. at the controls, came at Groom Lake on 30 April 1962.

The fist flight of YF-12A No. 1 came about at Groom Lake on 7 August 1963 with Lockheed Skunk Works test pilot James D. "Jim" Eastham in command.

In this nation, especially in the many vast areas of dry lakes and barren plains "in the middle of nowhere," there are most likely other secret places where classified air vehicles are being flight tested even as I write. And when one thinks of just how advanced Lockheed's series of trisonic Blackbird aircraft were in the early 1960s, one can only imagine what might be out there somewhere today, more than 40 years later. But most assuredly, when and if they are uncovered, they will surprise and maybe even shock us with their appearances, capabilities, and performances.

North American test pilot Vance Breese was in command of the first North American B-25 Mitchell prototype airplane during its first flight on 19 August 1940, from Inglewood to Muroc. It was powered by two air-cooled 1,700-horsepower Wright R-2600-9 Double Cyclone radial engines, which gave it a top speed of 322 miles per hour at 15,000 feet. It was 54 feet 1 inch long, 14 feet 10 inches high, and it had a wingspan of 67 feet 6 inches; gross takeoff weight was 23,715 pounds. So successful was B-25 in its early going the U.S. Army Air Corps (USAAC) was quick to order it into production. And it's a good thing it did, because during World War II the Mitchell excelled in every theater of combat operations. It is also famed for its use in the Doolittle Raid, in which 16 B-25Bs, which had launched off the carrier USS *Hornet*, first gave Japan a payback for Pearl Harbor when they bombed several Japanese cities, including Tokyo. All in all, close to 10,000 Mitchell bombers were built before production ended. Moreover, the U.S. Navy procured a number of them, which were designated PBJ, to serve as land-based patrol bombers. The first B-25 is shown after it landed at Muroc when it completed its first flight. *North American Aviation*

The first of 13 service test Lockheed YP-38 Lightning airplanes made its first flight at Burbank, California, on 17 September 1940, with Lockheed test pilot Marshall Headle at the controls. It had been preceded by the one-of-a-kind XP-38 on 27 January 1939. So successful were the YP-38s that Lockheed went on to produce more than 10,000 production P-38s and their F-4/F-5 photographic reconnaissance counterparts. During World War II, P-38s created no fewer than 78 aces with (at least five kills each), including America's top two aces, Richard Bong (40 kills) and Thomas McGuire (38 kills). The YP-38 was powered by two turbo supercharged 1,150-horsepower 12-cylinder liquid-cooled Allison V-1710-27 or -29 v-shaped piston engines, which gave it a top speed of more than 400 miles per hour. It was 37 feet 10 inches long, 12 feet 10 inches high with a wingspan of 52 feet 0 inches. *Lockheed Martin*

Lockheed YP-38
Lightning No. 2.
Lockheed Martin

14

The premier Curtiss Model CW-20T, soon designated C-46 and named Commando, made its first flight on 26 March 1940 at St. Louis, Missouri, with Edmund T. "Eddie" Allen at the controls. It was powered by two 1,600-horsepower Wright R-2600 Cyclone air-cooled radial engines. The CW-20T was 76 feet 4 inches long, 21 feet 9 inches high, with a wingspan of 108 feet 0 inches; gross weight was 45,000 pounds. Curtiss developed the C-46 as an alternate to the Douglas DC-3/C-47 series of aircraft. While it had its own fame as good transport, the C-46 never surpassed the fame generated by the DC-3/C-47 series. *U.S. Air Force*

Powered by two air-cooled 18-cylinder 1,850-horsepower Pratt & Whitney R-2800-5 Double Wasp radial engines, the premier Martin B-26 Marauder made a successful first flight at Baltimore, Maryland, on 25 November 1940, with Martin test pilot Ken Ebel in command. The early B-26s measured 58 feet 3 inches in length, 19 feet 10 inches in height, with a 65-foot wingspan. They had a maximum speed of 315 miles per hour, a ceiling of 23,500 feet and a range of 1,000 miles carrying 3,000 pounds of bombs. Early production B-26s suffered from aerodynamic problems because their wings were too short. This aerodynamic flaw was so bad, in fact, that the B-26 earned the nickname "Widow Maker." After their wingspan had been increased by 6 feet to 71 feet, the instability disappeared. The Marauder subsequently became one of the best medium-class bombers in World War II. *U.S. Air Force*

Curtiss XP-46.
U.S. Air Force

Two Curtiss XP-46 airplanes were ordered as possible Curtiss P-40 Warhawk replacements. The second XP-46, delivered first without armament and other equipment, was redesignated XP-46A, and it flew first on 15 February 1941. The first airplane, delivered with all-up equipment, remained XP-46 and it flew second on 29 September 1941. Since the XP-46A and XP-46 did not demonstrate that much of a performance increase over the P-40C already being produced, the U.S. Army Air Corps opted to order another version of the P-40 with the few P-46 improvements. This became the P-40D version of the Warhawk. The XP-46 was powered by a single inline liquid-cooled 1,150-horsepower Allison V-1710-29 V-12 piston engine. It was 30 feet 2 inches long, 13 feet high, and it had a wingspan of 34 feet 4 inches. Its armament comprised eight .30-caliber machine guns in the wings and two nose-mounted .50-caliber machine guns. Its top speed was 355 miles per hour at 12,300 feet. *U.S. Air Force*

The premier Lockheed C-69 Constellation made six inaugural test flights on 1 January 1943. On the first flight, piloted by Edmund T. "Eddie" Allen—on loan from Boeing—the airplane flew out of Burbank for 50 minutes before landing at Muroc Army Air Base (AAB). It flew another five times that day. The premier Connie was actually the prototype airliner that had been ordered by Trans World Airlines to compete against the Boeing Model B-307 Stratoliner. But the U.S. Army Air Forces had quickly realized its potential as a fast troop transport, and it was drafted into duty as the C-69. Shown is the eighth production C-69-1-LO, the ninth Connie built. After the war, most C-69s were converted by the airlines for use as originally intended. The first C-69s was 95 feet 2 inches long, 23 feet 8 inches high with a wingspan of 123 feet. They came with four air-cooled 2,200-horsepower Wright R-3350-35 18-cylinder radial engines, which gave them a top speed of 330 miles per hour. After the war, the Constellation, affectionately nicknamed "Connie," became the best piston-powered airliner in the world,—a reign it held until the advent of the Boeing 707, Convair 880, and Douglas DC-8 jetliners. (Famed engineering test pilot Eddie Allen was killed less than two months after he flew the premier Connie in the crash of the No. 2 Boeing XB-29 Superfortress at Seattle, Washington, on 18 April 1943.) *Lockheed Martin*

An early production C-69. *Lockheed Martin*

Developed under AMC Project MX-14, the XP-Northrop XP-56 was to be a high-speed interceptor pursuit optimized for the protection of the United States from enemy bombardment. Development problems with its contrarotating propellers, combined with aerodynamic problems caused by its very short and small-area vertical tail, spelled doom for the "Black Bullet." Two XP-56 aircraft were built, and the first example made its first flight—a very low ground-hugging test hop—at Muroc AAB on 6 September 1943 with Northrop test pilot John Myers in control. It crashed on 8 October 1943, but Myers survived. The less radical second example, featuring a larger vertical tail, made its first flight on 23 March 1944 with Myers at the controls. The XP-56 airplanes were powered by single 2,000-horsepower Pratt & Whitney R-2800-29 air-cooled radial engines. Production P-56s were to have a projected top speed of 465 miles per hour at 19,500 feet. They were relatively small pusher-type aircraft measuring 23 feet 7 inches in length, with a wingspan of 42 feet 7 inches with down-turned tips. They were in competition with two other pusher-type pursuits: the Consolidated-Vultee XP-54 Swoose Goose and Curtiss XP-55 Ascender. Neither of these designs fared any better than the XP-56, and they too were not proceeded with. *Garry Pape Collection*

XP-56
U.S. Air Force

The one-of-a-kind Douglas XB-19 made a successful first flight from Clover Field in Santa Monica, California, to March Army Air Field in Riverside, California, on 27 June 1941. Piloted by U.S. Army Air Forces Major Stanley M. Ulmstead, it was the world's largest bomber-type airplane to fly until the first flight of the Convair XB-36 on 8 August 1946. The XB-19, powered by four 18-cylinder, 2,000-horsepower Wright air-cooled R-3350-5 radial engines, was 132 feet 4 in long, 42 feet high and spanned 212 feet; its gross weight was 162,000 pounds. It was created from top secret Project D, which was started by the U.S. Army Air Corps in February 1935 as a long-range bomber plan "investigating the maximum feasible distance into the future." Sikorsky aircraft also offered up a design designated XBLR-1 (Experimental Bomber, Long Range-1) whereby Douglas got XBLR-2 (later designated XB-19). Douglas' design won, and it was built. Top speed of the XB-19 was 225 miles per hour at 15,700 feet. The re-engined XB-19A was powered by four 2,600-horsepower Allison V-3420-11 inline engines; top speed increased to 265 miles per hour at 20,000 feet. *U.S. Air Force*

In early 1944, North American Aviation (NAA) won a contract to build three XP-82 Twin Mustang airplanes for the U.S. Air Force. The first example made its first flight on 16 June 1945, piloted by NAA test pilot Joe Barton. It was powered by two 1,350-horsepower Packard V-1650 Merlin engines spinning counter-rotating propellers and had a top speed of 470 miles per hour. The third example, designated XP-82A, was powered by two 1,600-horsepower Allison V-1710 engines, also turning counter-rotating propellers. The second Merlin-powered example is shown, circa late 1945. Essentially two P-51H Mustang fuselages hooked together by a common wing and horizontal stabilizer, these double Mustang aircraft were thoroughly evaluated at Muroc in the mid- to late-1940s. The tests were successful and the Twin Mustang went into production as both a long-range fighter and night (all-weather) fighter. *North American Aviation*

The Douglas C-74 Globemaster I, the first very large-capacity-cargo transport airplane in the world, featured outward-opening doors and a ramp in its nose for ease of loading. The first of 14 service-test examples made its first flight of 1 hour and 35 minutes from Long Beach, California back to Long Beach on 5 December 1945. It was powered by four air-cooled 3,250-horsepower Pratt & Whitney R-4360-69 Wasp Major radial engines, which gave it a top speed of 330 miles per hour. It was 124 feet 2 inches long, 43 feet 9 inches, high with a wingspan of 173 feet 3 inches. A further development of the C-74 was the Douglas C-124 Globemaster II, which was produced in high quantity. The legacy of the Globemaster was carried on when McDonnell Douglas (now Boeing) named its C-17A the Globemaster III. *U.S. Air Force*

The first of two Republic XF-12A Rainbow airplanes made a successful first flight on 4 February 1946 at Farmingdale, Long Island, New York. It was piloted by Republic test pilot Lowery Brabham, chief test pilot; Oscar Hass, copilot; and James Creamer, flight test engineer. There is little doubt that the Republic XF-12-cum-XR-12 Rainbow was one of the most beautiful airplanes ever built. It was intended as a high-altitude, high-speed photographic reconnaissance and mapping platform. It remains the fastest multiengine, piston-powered, and propeller-driven airplane to fly, with its attained top speed of 450 miles per hour in level flight. The Rainbow was 98 feet 9 inches long, 29 feet 11 inches high, with a wingspan of 129 feet 2 inches. It was powered by four 3,000-horsepower air-cooled Pratt & Whitney R-4360-31 Wasp Major 28-cylinder radial engines. After the U.S. Air Force aircraft redesignation program took effect in June 1948, the XF-12 became known as the XR-12 (F for Photo gave way to R for Reconnaissance). *U.S. Air Force*

The first of two Northrop XB-35 airplanes made a successful first flight from Hawthorne to Muroc on 25 June 1946. It was piloted by Northrop test pilot Max Stanley. As a semi-all-flying-wing design, the XB-35 featured a wingspan of 172 feet. It was 53 feet 1 inch long and 20 feet 1 inch high; gross weight was 180,000 pounds. It was powered by four air-cooled 3,000-horsepower Pratt & Whitney R-3350-17 (or -21) radial engines, each spinning two propellers—one clockwise, one counterclockwise to eliminate torque. A number of follow-on YB-35s and B-35s were built, but due to their pronounced instability as bombardment platforms they were ultimately scrapped. Three of them, however, survived to become the two jet-powered YB-49s and the lone jet-powered YRB-49A. *Air Force Flight Test Center, Historian's Office, hereafter abbreviated as [AFFTC/HO]. Garry Pape Collection*

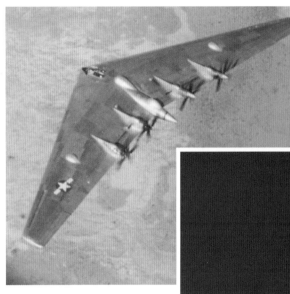

On 9 November 1946 the first of two Lockheed XR6O-1 Constitution airplanes made its first flight (2 hours, 17 minutes) from Lockheed Air Terminal in Burbank to Muroc AAB. It was piloted by Lockheed test pilot Joe Towel and copiloted by Tony LeVier. The second example made its first flight in June 1948. Constitution No. 1 was powered by four air-cooled 3,000-horsepower Pratt & Whiney R-4360-18 Wasp Major radial engines; it was later retrofitted with 3,500-horsepower-22Ws as was Constitution No. 2. The XR60-1 was of a double-deck design measuring 156 feet 1 inch in length, 50 feet 4 1/2 inches in height, with a wingspan of 189 feet 1 1/4 inches; gross weight was 184,000 pounds. *Lockheed Martin*

Convair test pilot Beryl A. Erikson piloted the XB-36 for 37 minutes during its first flight on 8 August 1946. Seven crewmembers and copilot G. S. "Gus" Green accompanied aircraft commander Erickson. The XB-36 was powered by six air-cooled 3,000-horsepower Pratt & Whitney R-4360-25 Wasp Major radial engines in a pusher rather than tractor arrangement; top speed was 346 miles per hour at 35,000 feet. When the XB-36 appeared at its 8 September 1945 rollout, it was easily the largest bomber-type plane ever built, measuring 162 feet 1 inch long, 46 feet 8 inches high, and its wingspan was 230 feet. The XB-36 was later re-engined with uprated 3,500-horsepower R-4360-41 Wasp Majors, and its single-wheel main landing gear was replaced with four-wheel bogies. It then became the YB-36A, and as such, made its first flight in June 1948. The Convair Division of General Dynamics Corporation went on to build 385 B-36s. Two of these, initially designated YB-36G, became the two eight-jet YB-60 airplanes discussed elsewhere. *Lockheed Martin via Dennis R. Jenkins*

Stanley Betz, pilot, and Roy Wimmer made a successful first flight of the premier Lockheed YC-130 Hercules on 23 August 1954 from Burbank to Edwards AFB. The YC-130 was powered by four 3,250-equivalentshaft-horsepower Allison T56-A-1 turboprop-jet engines, which gave it a top speed of 380 miles per hour at 20,400 feet. It is 97 feet 8 inches long, 38 feet 5 inches high with a wingspan of 132 feet 6 inches; gross weight was 124,200 pounds. Two YC-130s were built, and their respective flight test programs led to full-scale production of the C-130A and numerous follow-on versions of the workhorse Hercules transport, which is still in production as the C-130J. *Lockheed Martin*

The Vought model VS-315 or XF5U-1 "Flying Pancake" was a saucer-shaped, twin-engine, single-seat, low-aspect ratio flying-wing type of airplane, manufactured by the Chance Vought Division, United Aircraft Corporation, Stratford, Connecticut. The first of two XF5U-1 airplanes was used for static tests; proof loads, extended to ultimate, largely confirmed structural design predictions. The second XF5U-1 airplane was used for experimental flight test and concept validation. It was never flown because many hours of engine runup showed excessive mechanical vibration between the engine-propeller shafting, gear boxes, and airframe structure. The airplane was taxi tested by Chance Vought test pilot Boone Guyton on 3 February 1947 at Stratford, Connecticut, but, again, vibration levels were considered excessive. The XF5U-1 was powered by two 1,350-horsepower Pratt & Whitney R-2000-7 engines. It was 28 feet 1 1/2 inches long, 16 feet 8 inches high with a span of 23 feet 4 inches. The airplane was being readied for shipment by sea through the Panama Canal to Edwards AFB, California, when the contract was canceled because of still unsolved technical problems and the lack of Navy research and development money. *Ling-Temco-Vought*

Douglas test pilot J. C. Armstrong completed the first flight of the premier C-133A Cargomaster on 23 April 1956 at Long Beach, California. It was powered by four 7,000-horsepower Pratt & Whitney T34 turboprop-jet engines, which gave it a top speed of 350 miles per hour. It is 157 feet 6 inches long, 48 feet 8 inches high, and has a wingspan of 179 feet 8 inches; gross weight is 282,000 pounds. While the first C-133A served as a prototype, it did not receive an X or Y prefix. When the Cargomaster appeared, it was largest and heaviest transport in the world, even surpassing the size and weight of the Douglas C-124 Globemaster II. Douglas went on to build 50 Cargomaster transports: 35 C-133As and 15 C-133Bs. With the advent of the gigantic, jet-powered Lockheed C-5 Galaxy, the C-133s began to retire in 1971. *AFFTC/HO*

With Lockheed test pilot Jim Eastham at the controls, the first of three Lockheed YF-12A aircraft made its maiden flight on 7 August 1963 at Groom Dry Lake, Nevada. The YF-12A was to be an improved manned interceptor (IMI) and, in fact on 14 May 1965, the U.S. Air Force funded an F-12B version for production as the IMI. The U.S. Air Force—specifically, its Air Defense Command (ADC)—wanted 93 of them to be built, but on 5 January 1968 the F-12B program was abruptly canceled with little or no explanation. This was strange, because in tests the YF-12A demonstrated that the projected F-12B would have easily been the world's premier interceptor, period. To be armed with three heat-seeking Hughes AIM-47 Falcon air-to-air guided missiles with a range exceeding 100 miles, the proposed F-12B was to be used strictly as an all-weather interceptor capable of speeds and altitudes exceeding 2,000 miles per hour (Mach 3) and 80,000 feet. The three YF-12As were each powered by two 34,000-pound-thrust class Pratt & Whitney J58 turbojet engines. As interceptor-type aircraft, they were quite large, measuring 101 feet long, 18 feet 6 inches high, with a wingspan of 55 feet 7 inches. They were quite heavy as well, with a maximum takeoff weight of 127,000 pounds. *NASA*

On 25 April 1960 Lockheed test pilot Lou Schalk successfully completed a short first flight of the highly classified Lockheed A-12 at Groom Dry Lake on the Nellis AFB complex in southern Nevada. It only flew a distance of about 10,560 feet (roughly two miles) at a height of just 20 feet or so. An unofficial first flight of about 40 minutes followed the next day, on 26 April. The official first flight, with Central Intelligence Agency (CIA) and USAF personnel present, came on 30 April. Eventually, powered by two 32,500 pound-thrust class Pratt & Whitney J58 turbojet engines, the A-12s were hitting speeds of Mach 3.30 at 90,000 feet. The A-12 is 102 feet, 3 inches long, 18 feet, 6 inches high, with a wingspan of 55 feet 7 inches; gross weight was 117,000 pounds. Two A-12s, modified to carry D-21 reconnaissance drones, were redesignated M-21. *Lockheed Martin Skunk Works*

The Development of the Lockheed Constellation

On 30 November 1944, some 22 months after the first Constellation appeared in the skies over southern California, Lockheed chief research engineer Clarence L. "Kelly" Johnson presented a paper to the Los Angeles section of the Institute of Aeronautical Sciences. He discussed thoroughly the engineering, testing, and research on the basic design problems of a large transport airplane. Some highlights of his paper, which will clarify some misleading information found in other references on the "Connie," follow:

"The initial design studies for this airplane were first undertaken in June 1939. The Lockheed L-049 Constellation, known also by the U.S. Army Air Forces designation of C-69, was conceived as a long-range, high-speed, high-altitude transport, for which low operating cost was a basic requirement. The flight characteristics desired were to be a substantial improvement over those of existing aircraft, with maximum controllability available for all emergency, as well as normal, flight conditions.

"Designed from the outset as a four-engine transport plane, the first problem encountered concerned the size of the engine to be used. It soon became apparent that the best airplane for the task would be one equipped with very large engines, operating at a low percentage of their rated power, with the minimum possible degree of supercharging. Thus, we selected the 2,200-horsepower, 18-cylinder, air-cooled Wright R-3350-35 Double Cyclone radial engine, with a 3,350 cubic-inch displacement.

"The question is frequently asked why the fuselage shape of the Constellation is so unusual. The explanation is very simple. In order to reduce the length of the nose landing gear, which was already very long, due to the large diameter of the three-bladed propellers, the mean camber line of the fuselage was lowered for the forward section of the fuselage. To reduce the drag at the maximum lift-to-drag ratio of the plane, a slight downward curvature was also employed aft of the wing. This gave the fuselage a basic shape corresponding roughly to the mean flow line over the wing at cruising speed; result, reduced drag.

"The first flight of the Constellation took place on 9 January 1943. Previous to that date, extensive preparations had been made for complete flight testing on all components of the airplane. Having completed the preflight tests, the airplane was taken off and flown on six different flights the first day. After a 50-minute first flight, the airplane was landed at Muroc Army Air Field, and there, five more flights were made. No difficulty was experienced on these flights, so the formal flight test program was undertaken.

"On 17 April 1944 the first Constellation was flown at high altitude from Los Angeles to Washington, D.C., in an elapsed time of 6 hours, 57 minutes, 51 seconds. The Constellation is expected to repeat this type of performance in the future during its service with the U.S. Army Air Forces and later with the world's airlines."

— *Clarence L. Johnson*, Lockheed Martin

[The legendary Kelly Johnson, founder of the famed Skunk Works, is credited with the design of some 40 Lockheed aircraft, including the Constellation. Some of his other significant designs included the P-38 Lightning, F-80 Shooting Star, F-104 Starfighter, U-2, and the A-12/YF-12/SR-71 series of aircraft. After numerous years of faithful duty to Lockheed and his country, at the age of 80, he passed away on 21 December 1990.]

Clarence L. Johnson. *Lockheed Martin*

On 22 December 1964, with Lockheed test pilot Robert Gilliland at the controls, the first Lockheed SR-71A made a successful first flight at Palmdale, California. The SR-71A, known as the Blackbird, is powered by two afterburning 34,000-pound-thrust-class Pratt & Whitney J58 turbojet engines that give it a top speed of about Mach 3.3 at 90,000 feet. It is 107 feet 5 inches long, 18 feet 6 inches high with a wingspan of 55 feet 7 inches; gross weight is 170,000 pounds. Incidentally, on the very same day, but at Groom Dry Lake, Nevada—the so-called Area 51—the first M-21 "mother" and D-21 "daughter" captive carry flight occurred with Lockheed test pilot Bill Park at the helm. Two M-21 (M for Mother) air vehicles were created to carry the Mach 3-plus D-21 (D for Drone and/or Daughter) reconnaissance vehicles, which were launched from the back of the M-21s at high speed and high altitude. *Lockheed Martin Skunk Works*

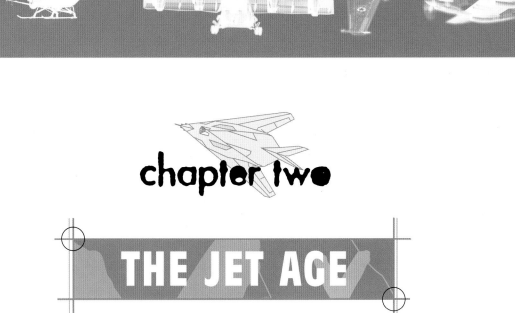

chapter two

THE JET AGE

THE FIRST USE of a turbojet (gas turbine) engine for a dedicated aircraft propulsion system occurred in Germany on 27 August 1939. The small 4,400-pound Heinkel Model He-178, powered by a single 838-pound thrust Heinkel S38 turbojet engine, was flown by Luftwaffe Captain Erich Warsitz on that day, and it easily exceeded 400 miles per hour. But the historic event was top secret, and it would be quite some time before the world knew that the Jet Age had arrived.

Then on 15 May 1941 another country flew an airplane powered by a turbojet engine. This was the Gloster Aircraft Model G.40 Pioneer, of Great Britain, which was powered by a single 860-pound thrust Power Jets Whittle W.1X turbojet engine, and it was flown by Royal Air Force Flight Lieutenant Philip E. G. "Jerry" Sayer. U.S. Army Air Corps Commander Henry H. "Hap" Arnold, who was most impressed to say the least, was in attendance for the historic flight. Upon his return to the United States, Arnold immediately set forth a program whereby America would develop a turbojet-powered aircraft.

Simultaneously, on 30 September 1941, Bell Aircraft Corporation and General Electric Company were awarded top-secret development contracts to manufacture airplanes and turbojet engines. Bell, under Secret Project MX-397, was contracted to build three Model 27 XP-59A airplanes, which were named Airacomet. General Electric was contracted to manufacture an adequate number of its Model I-A (pronounced "eye-A") turbojet engines based upon the W.2B, an outgrowth of the Whittle W.1X, to propel the Airacomets. This project was to be accomplished in one year's time, and amazingly, it was.

In September 1942 the first XP-59A and a pair of 1,250-pound-thrust I-A turbojet engines arrived at Muroc Army Air Base in railroad boxcars. The airplane quickly was assembled and the engines were installed; taxi tests began later that month.

Then, on 2 October 1942 the Jet Age began in America, when Bell Aircraft Corporation chief test pilot Robert M. "Bob" Stanley lifted off from the north end of Muroc Dry Lake and successfully flew the Bell XP-59A Airacomet. Several successful flights were made that day, and the last one was flown by Colonel Laurence C. "Bill" Craigie, head of the U.S. Army Air Forces experimental aircraft programs. Stanley had made several test hops the preceding day up to 100 feet high, but since no dignitaries were on hand to witness the events, the flights were considered to be unofficial.

Flying America's First Jet-Powered Airplane

In a letter to this writer dated 25 February 1991, General Laurence C. "Bill" Craigie shared his experience of becoming the first military pilot in America to fly a jet-powered airplane:

"Any mention of an X- or Y-model airplane immediately brings to mind the Air Force flight test center at Edwards Air Force Base, California. And, indeed, the center got a most dramatic start in 1942 when it was selected as the test site for the Bell XP-59A Airacomet, America's first turbojet-powered airplane. The center was then known as Materiel Center Flight Test Site and was selected because of its remoteness and its almost unlimited expanse of smooth, dry lake bed.

"It was my good fortune to be in charge of U.S. Army Air Forces experimental aircraft programs at the time the XP-59A came on the scene. I actually backed into the distinction of being the second American jet pilot because, when the XP-59A was ready for its assembly and flight testing at Muroc, Lieutenant Colonel Ralph Swofford, the project officer on the XP-59A program, was in England discussing turbojet propulsion system matters with the British. The British had a keen interest in our program in view of the fact that the XP-59A was powered by the I-A engine, an Americanized version of the original Whittle engine, which had powered their first jet, the Gloster G.40 Pioneer.

"The General Electric Company, the powerplant contractor, was quite conservative regarding the early operation of the XP-59A propulsion units. After all, the engines were far more experimental than the airframe. During those first few flights the pilot was limited to half-power. (We were curious as to just how much static [sea-level] pounds of thrust we were getting at half-power. Bob Stanley, Bell's chief test pilot, had his people drive a fence post into the lake bed, a spring scale was attached between it, and the airplane and the engines were opened up to the maximum General Electric would permit. The scale gave us a reading of 1,600 pounds thrust; that is, a mere 800 pounds thrust per engine!

"Moreover, the engines were limited to three hours' running time, including run-up, taxiing, and flight time, after which the engines were to be removed, partially disassembled and inspected to determine the effects of high temperature and wear on certain critical parts.

"The airplane was brought to Muroc from Bell's Buffalo, New York, facility by rail and arrived on 19 September 1942. Bob Stanley taxied the airplane on 1 October, actually getting it a few feet off the ground on several occasions. (Since the airplane did rise to 25, then 50, and finally about 100 feet that day, these were considered to be 'unofficial' first flights.)

"The 'official' first flight took place on 2 October. He followed this up with a second flight, after which he commented to me that only 25 minutes remained of the three hours' time we were allowed, and suggested that I fly the airplane. I had been living with the project all year and felt close to all aspects of it so that seemed like an excellent idea to me. I gladly accepted Bob's invitation.

"The flight itself was quite uneventful except for the high temperature in the cockpit due to a malfunction of the windshield and canopy glass defogging system. My clearest recollection of my flight in the XP-59A was the extreme quiet and complete lack of vibration as I took off. Of course,

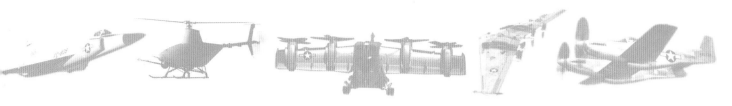

this was due in large part to the smooth rotary motion of the turbojet engines, as compared to the relatively rough and violent up and down motion of the conventional piston engines to which I was accustomed. The low takeoff power also contributed to the quietness.

"Thus, the turbojet engine, inherently more efficient at higher aircraft speeds, was the answer to the aircraft designer's prayer. The jet engine constituted a true breakthrough and opened up an entirely new era in aviation progress.

"And, in this country, it started with the Bell XP-59A Airacomet. Though not a combat-worthy machine—it was critically underpowered—it broke the ice, as it were, and introduced America to the Jet Age. And what an exciting and meaningful epoch the Jet Age has turned out to be!"
— *Laurence C. "Bill" Craigie,*
U.S. Air Force lieutenant general, retired
25 February 1991

[General Craigie was born in 1902 and passed away on 27 February 1994. He was 92. He was a true aviation and jet pioneer.]

Lieutenant General Lawrence C. Craigie
AFFTC/HO

Shown here is an in-flight view of the second of three Bell XP-59A Airacomet airplanes, with Bell test pilot Bob Stanley at the controls. The Bell XP-59A made its first "official" flight on 2 October 1942 at Muroc AAB. Powered by two 1,250–pound-thrust General Electric Model I-A (pronounced Eye-A) turbojet engines, the XP-59A struggled to hit its maximum speed of 404 miles per hour at 25,000 feet. The plane now is located in Washington, D.C., at the National Air and Space Museum. It is a most significant artifact because it was America's first jet-powered airplane. Combat P-59s were to have been armed with one 37-mm cannon and three .50-caliber machine guns—all nose-mounted. In addition to three prototype XP-59As, Bell built 13 service test YP-59As, 20 P-59As and 30 P-59Bs. The 60th anniversary of its first flight came recently, on 2 October 2002. *AFFTC/HO*

After the initial success of the flight, Bell was awarded another contract to develop a single-engine fighter, which became known as the XP-59B. Problems with its design arose, and the U.S. Army Air Forces looked to Lockheed Aircraft Corporation to come up with a better solution. So, under Secret Project MX-409, Lockheed won a contract to build a single Model L-140 airplane designated XP-80, which would be powered by a single 2,460-pound thrust de Havilland Halford Model H.1B Goblin turbojet engine. With Lockheed chief test pilot Milo Burcham at the controls, the XP-80 made a successful first flight at Muroc on 8 January 1944.

The experimental XP-80 fighter was agile and stable, and it exceeded 500 miles per hour. It was an immediate success, leading to orders for two prototype XP-80As and 13 service test YP-80A airplanes. These were designed with improved General Electric Model I-40 turbojet engines. The first XP-80A, flown by Lockheed test pilot Anthony W. "Tony" LeVier, made its first flight on 10 June 1944. (Milo Burcham had been killed in the crash of YP-80A No. 2 on 20 October 1944, and Tony LeVier subsequently took his place as chief test pilot.)

The Lockheed P-80 development program moved forward at a rapid pace, and the Shooting Star, as the P-80 was named, became the first operational jet-powered fighter in the U.S. Army Air Forces by the spring of 1945—too late for World War II action, but well in time for combat in the Korean War. (Bell's P-59 Airacomet had likewise entered U.S. Army Air Forces service, but only as a jet pilot transition and training aircraft, due its lack of performance and instability as a gun platform.)

While the Bell P-59 Airacomet and Lockheed P-80 Shooting Star programs were progressing, the U.S. Army Air Forces and U.S. Navy initiated a number of other jet-powered aircraft projects. These included several unsuccessful U.S. Army Air Forces entries, which included the following: the Northrop XP-79B, a proposed semiflying wing twin-jet interceptor; the Consolidated-Vultee XP-81 Silver Bullet, a proposed composite turboprop- and turbojet-powered fighter; and the Bell XP-83, a projected long-range fighter. The U.S. Navy also fielded several unsuccessful carrier-based fighter designs, which included the McDonnell FH-1 Phantom, the North American FJ-1 Fury, the Chance Vought F6U-1 Pirate, and the Ryan F2R-1 Dark Shark. However, one of the aforementioned, the FJ-2 Fury, in sweptback wing form, became the first operational jet fighter in the U.S. Navy.

These early turbojet-powered aircraft laid the stepping stones for many more new and advanced planes, including light and heavy attack bombers, bombers, fighters, transports, and unoccupied combat aerial vehicles. These have culminated in today's remarkable aircraft, such as the Lockheed Martin F/A-22 Raptor and F-35 Joint Strike Fighter, the Northrop Grumman B-2A Spirit, the Boeing C-17A Globemaster III, the Boeing X-45A, and the Northrop Grumman X-47A.

The No. 1 YP-59A is shown here with Bell test pilots Jack Woolams (cockpit) and Tex Johnston. *AFFTC/HO*

The Lockheed XP-80, nicknamed *Lulu-Belle*, was America's first 500-miles-per-hour jet-powered airplane. It was powered by a single 2,460-pound-thrust de Havilland Halford Model H.1B Goblin turbojet engine. With Lockheed test pilot Milo Burcham at the controls, it made its first flight on 8 January 1944. It proved to be everything the P-59 was not. That is, it was agile, fast, maneuverable, and a steady gun-firing platform. Built and flown in record time by what became the Skunk Works division of Lockheed Aircraft under Secret Project MX-409, the XP-80 was a success, leading to the development of the famed F-80 Shooting Star—America's first operational jet fighter. *Lulu-Belle* is shown here after being restored for permanent display at the National Air and Space Museum. *Lockheed Martin Skunk Works*

The XP-80A. *Lockheed Martin Skunk Works*

Two Lockheed XP-80A Shooting Star airplanes were built as an improved version of the XP-80 with a more powerful engine and improved features. They were both powered by single centrifugal-flow 3,750-pound-thrust General Electric J33-GE-11 turbojet engines, giving them a top speed of 560 miles per hour. The first example, with Tony LeVier at the controls, made its first flight at Muroc on 10 June 1944. The XP-80A was 34 feet 9 inches long, 11 feet 3 inches high, with a wingspan of 39 feet. So successful were these two service-test aircraft (albeit No. 1 crashed to destruction on 20 March 1945; LeVier bailed-out and survived) that Lockheed got a follow-on contract to build 13 further service-test YP-80A airplanes, forerunner to the production P-80As, America's first operational jet fighters. The YP-80As, except for being 1 inch longer, did not differ from the two XP-80As. For armament evaluations the XP-80As came with six nose-mounted .50-caliber machine guns. XP-80A No. 1 was nicknamed the *Gray Ghost* due to its paint scheme; No. 2, in bare metal, was known as the *Silver Ghost*. *Lockheed Martin Skunk Works*

The Douglas XB-43 holds the distinction of being America's first jet-powered bomber. Douglas test pilot Bob Brush made a successful first flight of the XB-43 at Muroc AAB on 17 May 1946. It was powered by two 4,000-pound-thrust General Electric J35-GE-3 turbojet engines mounted side-by-side within its fuselage; top speed was 515 miles per hour. The XB-43 was 51 feet 5 inches long and 24 feet 3 inches high, with a wingspan of 71 feet 2 inches; gross weight was 40,000 pounds. Although classified as a bomber, in all truthfulness the XB-43 was too small and light to meet that criterion. It was more of a light attack bomber, and with the current jet bomber developments, it quickly fell by the wayside. Still, according to Douglas Aircraft technical data, production B-43s were to carry up to 8,000 pounds of bombs. It was developed under AMC project MX-475, and its design was based on Douglas' earlier piston-powered XB-42 Mixmaster. *AFFTC/HO*

U.S. Air Force Major William Lien was the first test pilot to fly the premier North American XFJ-1 Fury–first of three examples, on 12 September 1946 at Muroc. The straight-winged XFJ-1 was 33 feet 5 inches long, 14 feet 10 inches high, and with its wing-tip fuel tanks, its wingspan was 39 feet 2 inches. The XFJ-1 was powered by a single nonaugmented 3,820-pound-thrust General Electric J35 turbojet engine; top speed was 542 miles per hour at 16,000 feet. Shown is an early production FJ-1, of which 30 examples was built to serve aboard the USS *Boxer* with VF-5A (later VF-51). With the adoption of sweptback wings to subsequent Fury models—FJ-2, FJ-3 and FJ-4— performance of the U.S. Navy Fury improved dramatically. These later models were based on U.S. Air Force F-86 Sabre Jets and became the navy's first swept-wing fighters. *North American Aviation*

North American Aviation built three XB-45 Tornado prototypes, and the first example made its first flight on 17 March 1947 at Muroc Air Force Base (AFB) with NAA test pilot George Krebs in command. These three model NA-130 airplanes were powered by four interim 4,000-pound-thrust class Allison-built General Electric J35-A-7 turbojet engines and had a top speed of 480 miles per hour at 30,000 feet. Some two months before the first XB-45 flew, on 20 January 1947, the U.S. Air Force ordered 96 production B-45A airplanes to be powered by four uprated 5,200-pound-thrust General Electric J47-GE-7 turbojet engines, which increased top speed to 500 miles per hour at 37,000 feet. The B-45A began to enter service with the U.S. Air Force Tactical Air Command in November 1948. Therefore, the Tornado became the first operational jet-powered bomber in America. *AFFTC/HO*

Three Douglas D-558-1 Skystreak aircraft were built for the U.S. Navy. Douglas test pilot Gene May flew the first example on its maiden flight at Muroc on 15 April 1947. The Skystreak was 38.71 feet long, 12.15 feet high, with a wingspan of 25 feet; gross weight was 10,105 pounds. It was powered by a single nonafterburning 5,000 pound-thrust-class Allison J35-A-11 turbojet engine. On two separate occasions just five days apart, the D-558-1 established new world-class speed records. The first one came on 20 August 1947, when U.S. Navy Commander Turner Caldwell attained 640.663 miles per hour. The second, on 25 August 1947, was set at 650.796 miles per hour by U.S. Marine Major Marion Carl. Skystreak No. 2 was lost in a crash on 4 March 1948, killing NACA test pilot Howard Lilly. *AFFTC/HO*

The Paperclip Flight

On 30 April 1966, pilot Alvin S. "Al" White [chief test pilot for North American Aviation's XB-70A] and myself [XB-70A test director for the U.S. Air Force] as copilot were to take the second of two XB-70A Valkyrie airplanes up for an assault on Mach 3.0, during which we were to fly over eight Western states [California, Oregon, Idaho, Montana, Wyoming, Utah, Nevada, and Arizona] in about 30 minutes. This was the 37th flight test of XB-70A No. 2 and the 30th time we had piloted one of the two air vehicles together.

Using 9,300 feet of runway at a takeoff weight of 530,000 pounds, we rotated at 202 knots indicated airspeed [KIAS, or 232.45 miles per hour] to become airborne. About 16 seconds after liftoff, I raised the handle to retract the landing gear. About 5–7 seconds after raising the handle, we heard a muffled *bang* and felt a *thump* within the airframe. I put the landing gear handle down. The main landing gear indicators were green, the nose gear green light was out, and the red light was illuminated. Major William J. "Pete" Knight, in a T-38 chase plane, reported the nose gear door had not opened far enough, and when the nose gear retracted, the door jammed between the twin nose gear wheels. He reported the nose gear was about halfway retracted and the left-hand nose gear tire had blown out.

As we orbited Edwards at a speed of 225 KIAS [258.9 miles per hour] and at an altitude of 9,000 feet, U.S. Air Force XB-70A test pilot Lieutenant Colonel Fitzhugh L. "Fitz" Fulton and NAA XB-70A test pilot Van H. "Shep" Shepard moved in closer with a chase TB-58A they were in and reported both main gear doors open, both bogies in their proper nose-up position.

The hydraulic landing gear sequence of operation called for the doors [some of which were closed with the gear extended] to open for gear retraction and then trigger an electrical switch to raise the gear. The nose gear door had failed to open fully, and the switch had not been triggered in a proper sequence. And even though the nose gear had been prompted to retract, the air pressure jammed its dual wheels up against the partially open door,

blowing the left-hand tire with explosive force. Thus the *bang* and *thump*.

Since the nose gear was jammed against the door, there was no way to retract it, nor extend it. Knowing this, if a cure couldn't be found, we knew we would have to prepare for an emergency ejection from the air vehicle after heading it for a remote gunnery range—and its crash to destruction, for the airplane's configuration simply would not allow for a landing without its nose gear down and locked. The nose gear, if not down and locked, would collapse on touchdown, and the XB-70A, with its very long nose, would break up.

We were now forced to circle Edwards while some North American engineers on the ground—Hal Smith and Bob McDonald, hydraulic engineers; Don Bickhart, electrical engineer; Frank Munds, flight test controller; and Walt Spivak, chief engineer—worked frantically to find a cure.

While we waited for a plan to be devised on the ground, I moved the landing gear emergency extend switch from *normal* to *all gear down*. The nose gear moved down about three inches and stopped, again indicating to the chase pilot that the nose gear door was the culprit. The main gear doors remained in place. I raised the canard foreplane flaps. When our speed increased to 285 KIAS (327.97 miles per hour), Al yawed the airplane out to four degrees left. There was no change. I returned the landing gear emergency extend switch to *normal*, and the nose gear moved up about six inches. I moved the same switch down again, and again, the nose came down three inches. Al yawed right three degrees. This, too, was ineffective. Nothing we tried seemed to work. We began to wonder if we'd be staying with the $500 million–plus airplane much longer.

Working with electrical circuitry diagrams, the engineers on the ground did in fact find a solution to our difficulty. They concluded that two very small pin terminals—among 15 in a small relay unit in the planes electronics bay—could be cross-circuited to *fool* the nose gear relay switch to extend the nose gear. But we didn't have their electrical diagrams.

I was told to go aft in the plane to the electronics bay and to open the relay unit panel so that I could draw a rough diagram of the relay unit and take it back to the cockpit. It was dark back there—without my flashlight (loaded with fresh Eveready batteries), I couldn't have pulled this off.

Lengthy radio conversations with the engineers on the ground ensued. After checks and rechecks, we, Al and I, were convinced we knew which two pin terminals to jump across. We had to figure out just how we were going to do that in a safe way, for the idea of jumping anything electrical isn't very popular with most of us.

I thought about using a paper clip as a jumper wire between the two close proximity pin terminals, which were only about one third of an inch apart. Al and the engineers on the ground agreed. But I still had to insulate myself from shock. After some thought, I decided to cut out a piece of seatbelt and

use it with a pair of pliers to grip the clip. Being nylon-based, the piece of safety belt would serve as a good insulator. At least I hoped so.

Holding my breath, I simultaneously touched the paper clip—which I had reshaped into the rough shape of a horseshoe—to the pin terminals.

Al lowered the gear handle, and then came the words from the chase pilots: "Gear coming down!" After I returned to the cockpit, I saw three green lights indicating that all gears were down and locked. Those three greens looked like a beautiful Christmas tree.

Our next problem was landing. Could the big airplane, still weighing some 307,000 pounds, be landed safely at almost 175 KIAS (201.4 miles per

continued

North American built three XP-86 Sabre Jet prototypes, and the first example made its first flight at Muroc AFB on 1 October 1947 with NAA test pilot George Welch at the controls. The XP-86 (redesignated XF-86 after June 1948) was the first sweptback winged airplane to fly in America. The original XP-86 Sabre Jet was 37 feet 6 inches long, 14 feet 9 inches high with a wingspan of 37 feet 1 inch; gross weight was 13,395 pounds. It was powered by a single 4,000 pound-thrust-class nonafterburning Chevrolet-built General Electric J35-C-3 (or -5) turbojet engine, which gave it a top speed 600 miles per hour. Production F-86s excelled in the Korean War, and when an F-86 downed a MiG-15, the war cry of the day was, "You've been 86ed!" That phrase has survived, is part of our daily jargon and can be heard today, and in many circles. *North American Aviation*

hour) with one of its nose gear tires flat? Could it be controlled on the landing roll?

A master pilot, Al decided to save enough fuel [i.e., not to dump most of it, as is standard during emergency landings] to land sufficiently fast to take off again if it appeared the blown-out tire was going to make the plane unmanageable upon the nose gear touchdown.

At the time we didn't know the malfunction had also locked six of the eight wheels on the main landing gear assemblies. That situation, in itself, made it a bail-out situation. Not only was one of the nose gear tires flat, but we would land and roll-out to a stop with only three of the 10 wheels turning. Now that I'm recalling the situation, I'm glad we didn't know about it.

With a great deal of finesse, Al landed the big airplane. As soon as the nose gear touched down, according to our chase pilots, the main gear burst into flames. And during the entire length of our 7,000-foot slide to a stop, the nose of the plane shook violently from side to side from the drag induced by seven nonrotating wheels and airless tires. The shake was so bad that the airplane's nose boom skipped around and broke.

Fortunately, even though we had landed at 172 KIAS (197.9 miles per hour), the airplane stayed relatively straight during the roll-out until it had came to a full stop, when it did veer to the right a bit. It had been two hours and 16 minutes since we had lifted off.

Damage to the air vehicle was mild, and on 16 May we took it back up for a check flight, which culminated with a speed run of Mach 2.73 at 65,000 feet. Three days later, we got to accomplish our goal of two earlier flights. That is, we flew over those eight Western states at a continuous speed of Mach 3 for 32 minutes at 72,500 feet.

But going back to the Paper Clip Flight, personally, I feel what could have been a real disaster had been diverted by a group of engineers and two pilots who had, for the most part, "grown-up" with the XB-70A Valkyrie—first, as a weapon system, and lastly, as a high-speed, high-altitude research airplane.

As an aside, through my own experience, it had become second nature for me to carry along a tool kit on test flights. In the kit I found all the tools I needed to apply corrective action within the pin terminal panel: that is, a flashlight with fresh batteries (it allowed me to see what I was doing), a pair of pliers, a slot-type screw driver, and a pair of diagonal cutters.

The all-important paper clip, a five-and-dime-store item, was holding together a half-inch-thick stack of flight-log papers.

— Colonel Joseph F. "Joe" Cotton (U.S. Air Force, retired)

[When the XB-70A flight test program ended on 4 February 1969, Joe Cotton had flown as pilot 19 times and copilot for 43 times; Al White had flown as pilot 49 times and copilot for 18 times. XB-70A flight test pilots "Fitz" Fulton and Van Shepard, the TB-58A chase plane crew during the Paper Clip Flight, respectively piloted the aircraft 31 and 23 times, and copiloted the aircraft 32 and 23 times.]

Colonel Joseph F. Cotton (left) and Alvin S. White.
North American Aviation

Two Northrop YB-49 Flying Wing Bomber service test airplanes were created from two highly modified XB-35s. The first example, piloted by Northrop test pilot Max Stanley, made its first flight—Hawthorne to Muroc—on 21 October 1947. It was powered by eight 3,750–pound-thrust-class nonafterburning Allison J35-A-15 turbojet engines, which gave it a top speed of 493 miles per hour at 20,800 feet. It was 53 feet 1 inch long, 15 feet 2 inches, and as a flying wing, it spanned 172 feet; gross weight was 193,940 pounds. The second YB-49 first flew on 13 January 1948 but was lost in a mysterious crash on 5 June 1948, killing its entire crew including its pilot, U.S. Air Force Captain Glen Edwards, for whom Edwards AFB is named. The first YB-49 was also lost due to a high-speed taxiing accident in March 1950. *AFFTC/HO*

With Boeing test pilot Robert Robbins in control, the first of two Boeing XB-47 Stratojet airplanes made a successful first flight from Seattle to Moses Lake, Washington, on 17 December 1947. The second example flew on 21 July 1948. It had received 5,200-pound-thrust General Electric J47-GE-3 engines prior to its first flight, and with these more powerful engines, it easily exceeded 600 miles per hour. In fact, it was faster than most jet fighters of the era. This sweptback-winged six-jet beauty was the forerunner of more than 2,000 production B-47s for Strategic Air Command (SAC). The XB-47 was powered by six 2,750-pound-thrust General Electric J35-GE-7 turbojet engines, which gave it a top speed of 578 miles per hour at 15,000 feet. The XB-47 Stratojet is 107 feet 6 inches long, 27 feet 8 inches high with a wingspan of 116 feet. *U.S. Air Force via Stan Piet*

Northrop test pilot Fred Bretcher made a successful first flight of the one-of-a-kind Northrop XF-89 Scorpion at Edwards AFB on 16 August 1948. Two XF-89s were to be built, but the second example was completed as the one-off service test YF-89A. The XF-89 was 50 feet 6 inches long, 17 feet 8 inches high with a wingspan of 52 feet; gross weight was 43,910 pounds. It was powered by two nonafterburning 4,000-pound-thrust Allison J35-A-15 turbojet engines and had a top speed of 600 miles per hour. The YF-89A made its first flight on 15 November 1949 and was powered by two afterburning 6,800-pound-thrust Allison J35-A-21A turbojet engines, which gave it 600 miles per hour speed. Flight testing of the XF-89 and YF-89A airplanes was successful, and the Scorpion entered service as a two-place night (all-weather) fighter. Shown is the one-of-a-kind XF-89. *AFFTC/HO*

Under the U.S. Air Force's parasite fighter program in the late 1940s, McDonnell built two XF-85 Goblin airplanes. Eventually, as projected, production F-85s would be carried by Convair B-36s to act as onboard escort fighters. From the belly of B-29 mother ship nicknamed *Monstro*, piloted by McDonnell test pilot Edwin Schoch, the second of two Goblins made its first free flight on 23 August 1948 at Edwards AFB. It was not until 8 April 1949 that the No. 1 XF-85 made its first (and only) free flight; the Parasite Program was canceled immediately afterward. Nicknamed Bubble Bee by those closely associated with it, the XF-85 measured 14 feet 10.5 inches in length, 8 feet 3 inches in height and spanned 21 feet 1.5 inches. Essentially a flying engine nacelle with wings, the Goblin was powered by a single nonafterburning 3,000-pound-thrust Westinghouse J34-WE-22 turbojet engine. Shown is the No. 1 XF-85 with test pilot Schoch. *AFFTC/HO*

McDonnell Aircraft built two XF-88 Voodoo prototypes for the U.S. Air Force penetration fighter program. Piloted by McDonnell test pilot Bob Edholm, the first XF-88 made its maiden flight at St. Louis on 20 October 1948. As originally flown, the XF-88 was woefully underpowered. But when it was retrofitted with two afterburning 4,200-pound-thrust Westinghouse J34-WE-15 turbojet engines and redesignated XF-88A, its performance improved to 641 miles per hour. The XF-88A was 54 feet 1.5 inches long, 17 feet 3 inches high with a wingspan of 39 feet 8 inches; gross weight was 18,500 pounds. The XF-88A defeated both the Lockheed XF-90A and North American YF-93A in a fly-off competition 29 June–11 July 1950. But by then, there was no longer a need for a fighter of that type. Ultimately, however, the F-88 metamorphosed into the F-101 Voodoo. *U.S. Air Force*

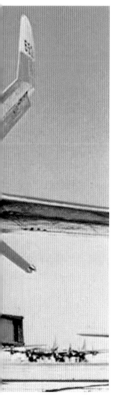

The one-of-a-kind Convair XF-92A Dart made its first flight on 18 September 1948 at Edwards AFB, with Convair test pilot Sam Shannon in command. The Dart, as it was nicknamed, was powered by a single afterburner-equipped 7,500-pound-thrust Allison J33-A-23 turbojet engine. It was 42 feet 6 inches long and 17 feet 9 inches high, with a wingspan of 31 feet 4 inches; gross weight was 14,610 pounds. The success of the XF-92A led to the development of the delta-winged B-58 Hustler, F-102 Delta Dagger, F-106 Delta Dart and F2Y Sea Dart—all built by the Convair division of General Dynamics. *AFFTC/HO*

Thoughts on the XB-70A Valkyrie

The XB-70A Valkyrie, built by North American Aviation under contract to the U.S. Air Force, is the only very large plane (fueled, it weighed more than 500,000 pounds) to be built that could fly more than three times the speed of sound (2,000 miles per hour). Originally designed as a dedicated weapon system, the plane was flown only to obtain research data, and it provided much valuable information during the U.S. Air Force test program and later during the NASA test program.

I was privileged to be part of the original team of four test pilots who were assigned to the program long before the first flight in September 1964. That pilot team was Al White and Van Shepard of North American Aviation and Colonel Joe Cotton and myself of the U.S. Air Force. When NASA took over on the XB-70A test program in 1967, I joined NASA and became the NASA chief project pilot on the air vehicle.

The Valkyrie was a unique airplane. It is very large; it has beautiful lines, and it is constructed primarily of stainless steel. The data gathered during its flight test programs has provided a vast pool of knowledge that has been used and is still being used in the design of other aircraft. The outstanding Rockwell [now Boeing North American] B-1B Lancer bomber has many design features that were first tried on the XB-70A. It only takes a quick look into the B-1B cockpit to see a few of them.

Two Northrop X-4 Bantam airplanes were built to explore flight by semitailless aircraft. Northrop test pilot Charles Tucker made the first flight of X-4 No. 1 at Muroc on 16 December 1948. It was powered by two nonafterburning 1,600-pound-thrust Westinghouse J30-WE-7 (or -9) turbojet engines, and its top speed was 640 miles per hour. The X-4 is 23 feet 3 inches long, 14 feet 10 inches high and it has a wingspan of 26 feet 10 inches; gross weight was 7,550 pounds. The second X-4 made its first flight on 7 June 1949. The X-4s were flown by the U.S. Air Force a number of times (30 flights) before they were turned over to NACA for ongoing flight test evaluations (60 flights). As it was designed and built, the Bantam (also known as the Skylancer) had no horizontal tail plane. Instead, for its pitch control, it had large area split flaps on the trailing edge of its wings; its large wings offered horizontal stability. *NASA*

The XB-70A was designed and manufactured by an outstanding team of people. The U.S. Air Force, NASA, and many contractor flight test teams were just as outstanding. The top quality people on the program . . . stand out in my mind when I think back about the program.

The XB-70A was not a particularly difficult airplane for experienced test pilots to fly. It was, however, an airplane that had different systems and different flying characteristics than any other airplane. The pilots had to be very knowledgeable about the airplane and prepared to handle any emergencies if and when they occurred. Witness the Paper Clip Flight. Even though it was a very large and heavy airplane, the two pilots were the only people on board. Engineers and technicians in the control room could, and often did, provide valuable information by radio, but the pilots had to make the final decisions and solve the problems.

There were many highlights and emotional highs on the program when things were done for the first time and major milestones were accomplished. There were also some very sad times, as when two of the ground crew were seriously hurt during a fueling operation. Both were to eventually die from their injuries. It was also a very sad day when XB-70A No. 2 was lost after a midair collision on 8 June 1966. Its copilot, U.S. Air Force Major Carl S. Cross, on his first XB-70A flight, was killed along with NASA test pilot Joe Walker in the F-104 escort plane; its pilot, Al White, though injured, survived.

A total of 129 flight test missions were flown on the two XB-70A air vehicles [83 for XB-70A-1 and 46 for XB-70A-2]. The final flight test phase on the program was conducted by NASA between early 1967 and February 1969. Don Mallick of NASA and Colonel Ted Sturmthal of the U.S. Air Force joined me as the pilots of XB-70A No. 1 during that series of flights. I flew as pilot on the last flight of the last surviving XB-70A from Edwards Air Force Base to the Air Force Museum at Dayton, Ohio; that was 4 February 1969. Ted Sturmthal was copilot and Don Mallick flew along side in the TB-58A escort airplane. The air vehicle, the largest and heaviest to ever fly at three times the speed of sound, is on permanent display there and is about to enjoy the 40th anniversary of its first flight [21 September 2004].

— Lieutenant Colonel Fitzhugh L. "Fitz" Fulton Jr. (U.S. Air Force, NASA, retired)

[Fitz Fulton, for all his aerospace-related accomplishments through more than four decades, has been for the most part ignored. But this is partially due to his quiet and humble nature. Never really wanting his "name in lights," Mr. Fulton is a true gentleman and a credit to his U.S. Air Force and NASA flight test pilot peers. Having served in the U.S. Air Force for 22 years, he joined NASA to serve yet another 20 years. Fulton, during his two full careers, has flown everything from the T-6 Texan to the SR-71 Blackbird. Whether a single-engine or multiengine airplane, or a piston-powered, propeller-driven, or turbojet-powered airplane, he just flew them. And he flew them well.]

Lieutenant Colonel Fitzhugh L. Fulton Jr.
AFFTC/HO

Republic test pilot Carl Bellinger made a successful maiden flight of the first of two XF-91 Thunderceptor airplanes at Edwards AFB on 9 May 1949. The Thunderceptor was a proposed high-speed, high-altitude, daytime area- and point-interceptor to be armed with four 20-mm cannon. It featured a composite propulsion system, the final configuration of which incorporated a single afterburning 7,500-pound-thrust General Electric J47-GE-17 turbojet engine and a single four-chamber 6,000-pound-thrust Reaction Motors XLR11-RM-9 rocket motor. With this propulsive system the XF-91 is credited with the distinction of being the first nondedicated X-type of aircraft to exceed the speed of sound. This event occurred on 9 December 1952 at Edwards AFB, when Republic test pilot Russell Roth hit Mach 1.07 in level attitude flight at 35,000 feet. The XF-91 is 43 feet 3 inches long, 18 feet 1 inch high and it has a wingspan of 31 feet 3 inches; gross weight was 28,300 pounds. The Thunderceptor featured inverse-tapered wings, which are wider at the tips than their roots. XF-91 No. 2 also featured a butterfly-type V-tail. *Ginter Books*

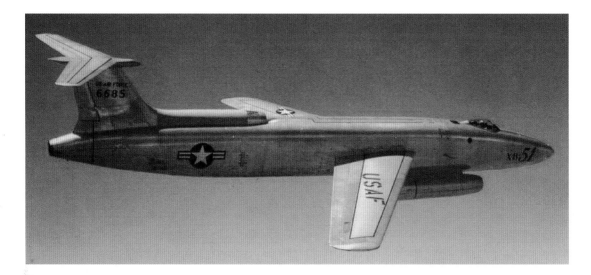

Formerly known as the XA-45, the first of two Martin XB-51 Panther prototypes made its first flight on 28 October 1949 at Baltimore, Maryland. It was piloted by Martin test pilot Pat Tibbs. The No. 2 XB-51 made its first flight on 17 April 1950. The XB-51 was powered by three nonafterburning 5,200-pound-thrust General Electric J47-GE-13 turbojet engines, top speed was 645 miles per hour. The Panther was 85 feet 1 inch long, 17 feet 4 inches high with a wingspan of 53 feet 1 inch; gross weight was 59,467 pounds. Both XB-51s were lost in crashes blamed on pilot errors. But one of them, with XF-120 emblazoned upon its nose as the "Gilmer XF-120 fighter," was featured in the 1956 movie *Toward the Unknown*, starring William Holden, which was filmed at Edwards AFB. The No. 2 XB-51 was lost at Edwards on 9 May 1952; the No. 1 was lost on 25 March 1956 at Biggs Field, Texas. *AFFTC/HO*

Two Lockheed XF-90 airplanes competed against the two McDonnell XF-88 Voodoo and two North American YF-93A Sabre Cat airplanes in the U.S. Air Force Penetration Fighter program. The first XF-90 made its maiden flight at Muroc on 3 June 1949 with Lockheed test pilot Tony LeVier at the controls. Both XF-90 airplanes were retrofitted with afterburning 4,200-pound-thrust Westinghouse J34-WE-15 turbojet engines, and top speed increased to 688 miles per hour. After their retrofit they were redesignated XF-90A. The Superstar, as the aircraft had been nicknamed, was 56 feet 2 inches long, 15 feet 9 inches high and had a wingspan of 40 feet; gross weight was 31,060 pounds. During the time period of 1 through 20 May 1950, LeVier performed 15 supersonic dive sorties, and on 17 May 1950 he power-dived the XF-90A to a maximum speed of Mach 1.12. As it turned out, the XF-90A was the XF-88A's closest rival, but like the XF-88A, it was never the penetration fighter the U.S. Air Force had been looking for. *Lockheed Martin Skunk Works*

Lockheed test pilot Tony LeVier made the first flight of the Lockheed YF-94C Starfire at Edwards on 19 January 1950; two were built and flown. Formerly designated YF-97A, the YF-94C was 44 feet 6 inches long, 14 feet 11 inches high, with a wingspan of 42 feet 5 inches; gross weight was 18,300 pounds. It was powered by an afterburning 8,750-pound-thrust Pratt & Whitney J48-P-5 turbojet engine, which gave it a maximum level-flight speed of 580 miles per hour. YF-94C tests were successful, and the type went into production as the F-94C Starfire. In December 1950, LeVier dove one of the YF-94C airplanes from 45,000 feet to supersonic speed as it passed through 33,000 feet. It therefore became the first straight-winged airplane in the world to exceed the speed of sound, other than the Bell X-1 rocket-powered airplane. *Lockheed Martin Skunk Works*

Recalling the F-8 Crusader Program

The Crusader was born as a result of a design competition held by the U.S. Navy Bureau of Aeronautics for a supersonic day fighter [that had] a desired speed of Mach 1.2 at altitude, was as light as possible, and, of course, was capable of operating from aircraft carriers.

Chance Vought Aircraft (now LTV Aerospace and Defense Company), proposed a unique design to these rather simply stated navy requirements. The airplane was about 55 feet long, with a wingspan of some 35 feet. The wing, with a five percent thickness ratio and 42-degree sweep-back, was shoulder mounted on the fuselage and contained about half of the fuel supply. A two-position wing was engineered to provide adequate vision over the nose at low speeds and yet have a high fineness ratio for high-speed flight. Both leading- and trailing-edge devices were incorporated and operated in conjunction with the wing position. The original engine was the Pratt & Whitney J57-P-11, which delivered about 15,000 pounds thrust. Subsequent engine dash numbers used in the Crusader gave up to 20,000 pounds thrust. The aft fuselage section was built of titanium alloy as a compromise to weight. Many other systems in the airplane were chosen to keep the airframe light as possible. The net result was an airframe which, when filled with 8,200 pounds of fuel, weighed slightly less than 25,200 pounds at takeoff. This was exceptional when compared to the U.S. Air Force Century Series of fighter aircraft.

The two prototype XF8U-1 aircraft produced speeds slightly over Mach 1.5 at 35,000 feet in their original configurations. The last F-8 model, the F-8E, was capable of speeds exceeding Mach 1.9 at altitudes above 57,000 feet. The designed maximum equivalent airspeed was 800 knots. The demonstrated maximum was more than 1,000 knots.

There were nine models of the Crusader produced. All of these designs were similar. The F8U-3 Crusader III was big brother to the F8U-1 Crusader I and F8U-2 Crusader II, bearing a similar appearance to the casual observer, but it was quite a different airplane. The Dash III was powered by the Pratt & Whitney J75 turbojet engine and weighed about 35,500 pounds at takeoff. Its full potential was never determined due to a foreshortened flight test program. However, the Crusader III did achieve altitudes above 70,000 feet and speeds above Mach 2.3 in October 1958.

John W. Konrad,
chief test pilot
15 April 1988

[John W. Konrad joined Chance Vought Aircraft in 1953 after leaving the U.S. Air Force with the rank of captain. He went to work with CVA as an experimental test pilot and began flying structural F7U-3 Cutlass demonstrations. He became CVA's chief test pilot a few months later and subsequently began work in the Crusader program. He became director of flight operations in 1964, then program manager of A-7 Corsair II special projects in 1983. I asked Konrad what his favorite model of the Crusader was. He replied, "The F8U-3 in its final configuration was my favorite. It had more acceleration, level flight speed, climb ability, and agility than any other plane I have flown. Its large internal fuel capacity and wonderfully coordinated flight control system allowed super flexibility." Konrad logged about 1,000 flight hours in various Crusader aircraft, and he last flew one in 1968. The highest Mach numbers and altitudes he attained in the Dash I, Dash II and Dash III Crusader models are: 1.60 Mn and 54,000 feet, Dash I; 1.92 Mn and 61,000 feet, Dash II; and, 2.32 Mn and 73,000 feet in a Dash III.]

John W. Konrad. *LTV*

The premier pilotless Chance Vought XSSM-N-8 Regulus cruise missile made its first successful test launch on 22 November 1950 at Edwards AFB. The XSSM-N-8 was 34 feet 4 inches long, 8.3 inches high with a wingspan of 21 feet 0 inches; gross weight was 13,810 pounds. It was powered by a single nonafterburning 4,600-pound-thrust Allison J33-A-14 turbojet engine which gave it a top cruising speed of 540 miles per hour over a distance of 520 miles at an altitude of 35,000 feet. Production Regulus cruise missiles carried nuclear warheads and were launched at sea by U.S. Navy submarines such as the USS *Growler* and USS *Grayback*. They became operational in 1955, and some 540 examples were built. They were later superseded by the Regulus II. *AFFTC/HO*

Douglas test Bob Rahn completed the first test flight of the premier delta-winged XF4D-1 Skyray at Edwards AFB on 23 January 1951. It initially was powered by a single nonafterburning 5,000-pound-thrust Allison J35-A-17 turbojet engine. It is 45 feet 8 inches long, 13 feet 0 inches high, with a wingspan of 33 feet 6 inches; gross weight was 26,000 pounds. Updated later with the addition of an afterburning 11,600-pound-thrust Westinghouse J40-WE-8 turbojet engine, the No. 2 XF4D-1 established a world speed record of 753-plus miles per hour. Douglas went on to produce 419 Skyray aircraft, and the last one was completed at Douglas' El Segundo plant in 1958. *Douglas Aircraft Company*

Two Bell X-5 airplanes were built, and the first example made its maiden flight at Edwards AFB on 20 June 1951 with Jean Ziegler at the controls. The X-5 aircraft were used to evaluate variable-geometry or swing-wings in flight. The X-5 was powered by a single nonafterburning 4,900-pound-thrust Allison J35 turbojet engine which gave it a top speed near 700 miles per hour. It is 33 feet 4 inches long, 12 feet 0 inches high with a fully extended wingspan of 32 feet 9 inches; 22 feet 8 inches swept back. The second example crashed to destruction on 13 October 1953; test pilot U.S. Air Force Major Raymond Popson was killed. The first example survives today at the Air Force Museum. The X-5 holds the distinction of being the world's first flying variable-geometry-winged airplane. *AFFTC/HO*

Famed test pilot Tex Johnston took the YB-52, shown in this photo, up for its first test flight on 15 April 1952 from Seattle to Moses Lake, Washington. The YB-52 flew before the XB-52 because the latter had received damage during ground testing. The XB-52 was repaired, and it flew on 2 October 1952—about one year late. The YB-52 was powered by eight 8,700-pound-thrust YJ57-P-3 turbojet engines, which gave it a top speed of 611 miles per hour at 20,000 feet. The YB-52 was 152 feet 8 inches long, 48 feet 3.6 inches high, with a wingspan of 185 feet. Its gross takeoff weight was a whopping 405,000 pounds. The success of the XB-52 and YB-52 airplanes led to the production of 742 additional Stratofortess aircraft in eight versions. The last version, the turbofan-jet-powered B-52H, 102 of which have been built, still soldiers on today, more than 40 years after its first flight on 6 March 1961. *U.S. Air Force*

Temporarily designated YB-36G, the YB-60 was an attempt by Convair to sell an eight-jet long-range strategic heavy bomber to the U.S. Air Force's Strategic Air Command. Two were built, and the first example made its first flight at Fort Worth, Texas, on 18 April 1952 (three days after the Boeing YB-52). It was powered by eight nonafterburning 9,000-pound-thrust Pratt & Whitney J57-P-3 turbojet engines, which gave it a top speed of 450 miles per hour—far short of the 600 miles per hour reached by the YB-52. Essentially an all-jet-powered B-36 with swept-back flying surfaces, the YB-60 was 171 feet long with a wingspan of 206 feet; gross weight was to be 410,000 pounds. Far and away, the B-52 was better than the B-60, and both YB-60s were eventually scrapped. *U.S. Air Force*

On 19 May 1952 Grumman test pilot Corwin Meyer successfully completed the first flight of the U.S. Navy swing-wing XF10F-1 Jaguar at Edwards AFB. It was powered by a single afterburning 10,900-pound-thrust Westinghouse J40-WE-8 turbojet engine, which gave it a top speed of 710 miles per hour. It is 54 feet 5 inches long, 16 feet 3 inches high and has a fully extended wingspan of 50 feet 7 inches; 36 feet 8 inches swept back. A number of swing-type aircraft had been built and flown, but it was not until the advent of the Grumman F-14 Tomcat that the U.S. Navy got its first operational variable-geometry airplane. The U.S. Air Force, on the other hand, got its first operational swing-wing when the General Dynamics F-111A went into service. Two XF10F-1 Jaguar airplanes were built, and even though Meyer made a number of successful flights—he was the only pilot to ever fly the Jaguar—the type was not acceptable, and the projected production F10F-1 was canceled. *AFFTC/HO*

On 20 October 1952 Douglas test pilot Bill Bridgeman made a successful first flight of the one-of-a-kind X-3 Stiletto at Edwards AFB. This stubby-winged air vehicle was originally intended to investigate double-sonic flight, whereby aerodynamic heating could be evaluated. But it was never adequately powered to attain such speeds, and it served as a test bed for short-span wings instead. It was powered by two afterburning 4,900-pound-thrust Westinghouse J34 turbojet engines, which ultimately gave it a top speed of just under Mach 1. It is 66 feet 10 inches long, 12 feet 6 inches high, and it has a wingspan of 22 feet 8 inches; gross weight is 22,400 pounds. Information gathered during flight tests of the X-3 was later incorporated in the wing design of the Lockheed XF-104 Starfighter, which in itself had an almost identical wingspan of 21.94 feet. *NASA*

Two North American YF-100 Super Sabre airplanes were built, and the first example made its maiden flight at Edwards on 25 May 1953 with North American test pilot George Welch in command. It was powered by a single afterburning 13,200-pound-thrust Pratt & Whitney J57-P-7 turbojet engine, and it went supersonic in level flight on its first test flight. It is 47 feet 1 1/4 inches long, 16 feet 3 inches high, and has a wingspan of 36 feet 7 inches; gross weight was 24,790 pounds. As its name implies, the Super Sabre was developed to supersede the North American F-86 Sabre of Korean War fame. The YF-100s proved successful in their respective flight test programs, and the Super Sabre went into production as the first in the series of U.S. Air Force Century Fighters. One version, known initially as the F-100B, became the double-sonic F-107A "Ultra Sabre." *AFFTC/HO*

The Lockheed F-104 Starfighter was the world's first production doublesonic fighter. Even in its experimental phase, powered by an interim afterburning 10,500-pound-thrust Wright YJ65-W-6 turbojet engine, the first of two XF-104s – first flown on 28 February 1954 at Edwards AFB by Lockheed test pilot Tony LeVier, reached a top speed of Mach 1.79. The XF-104 was 49 feet 2 inches long, 13 feet 5 inches high with an extremely limited wingspan of just 29 feet 9 inches. When LeVier first saw the XF-104, nicknamed "the missile with a man in it," he was quoted as asking its designer, Kelly Johnson, "Where's the goddamn wings?" Lockheed went on to produce and thoroughly wring out 17 service test YF-104As before it was allowed to manufacture the highly advanced Starfighter in production quantities. Shown is the second XF-104 prior to its crash to destruction on 18 February 1955; Lockheed test pilot Herman Salmon survived that crash. *Lockheed Martin Skunk Works*

Convair test pilot Richard Johnson was at the controls during the first flight test of the Convair YF-102 Delta Dagger at Edwards AFB on 24 October 1953. Developed under Weapon System 201A, the Delta Dagger was the world's first operational delta-winged interceptor. The YF-102 was powered by a single afterburning 14,500-pound-thrust Pratt & Whitney J57-P-11 turbojet engine. It was 52 feet 6 inches long, 18 feet 2 inches high with a wingspan of 38 feet 1 inch; gross weight was 26,400 pounds. The 11th service test YF-102 was modified to incorporate the NACA (now NASA) Area Rule configuration, whereby its fuselage was pinched in to allow drag-reducing airflow in and around its wing roots. Redesignated YF-102A, with this improvement it could exceed the speed of sound in level flight, while the earlier YF-102 could not. Ten YF-102s and four YF-102As were built before the F-102A shown entered into production and then service. *Lockheed Martin*

Flying the Grumman X-29

I have had the opportunity to fly most fighter-type aircraft and feel very fortunate. As well you well know, being in the right place at the right time has much to do with being selected for such activities. As director of advanced programs for U.S. Air Force/TAC [McCloud flew X-29A No. 1 during this assignment], I found myself in a position where it was important to me to understand emerging technologies firsthand. The best way to do that is to fly an aircraft such as the X-29 (or AV-8B, or F-16 LANTIRN), if the system is that far along. I've had other jobs of a similar nature in the past that opened doors like this. It's been extremely challenging, rewarding, and great fun!

As to comparing the forward-swept wing X-29 directly with the F-104, F-106, F-4, F-5, and other aircraft I've flown, I have some difficulty. First, the superb fly-by-wire flight control system of the X-29 masks some of the feel we had in older systems. That is, the F-4, for example, felt big and solid. Given a fly-by-wire flight control system, you can make the aircraft feel any way you wish. Sometimes feel can give you wrong impressions when comparing aircraft. Secondly, it's been some time since I flew last-generation aircraft, and the memory is probably dulled. Keep in mind that to really compare complex systems such as these, you must look at hard data, including energy [speed] maneuverability diagrams.

Overall, the X-29 seemed to hang on to energy better than other aircraft I have flown. This seemed most apparent at the higher G-loads and angles of attack, where last-generation aircraft were all, in a relative sense, energy losers. I felt that one of the high points of the X-29 was how far its flight control system had come in a short time . . . 241 flights [McCloud flew flight 241 out of 242 flights flown on X-29A No. 1 on 8 December 1988]. It was easy to transition to the X-29, and after 20 minutes I was comfortable,

even at higher G-loads. This says a great deal for the quality engineers and test pilots that tuned this unique system. Both of these characteristics are very important to nontest pilots, i.e., operational fighter pilots. We are always looking for aircraft that sustain energy at high-G . . . that are easy to handle, especially at maximum performance. The X-29 fell into this category.

— Colonel David J. McCloud,
10 May 1990

[David J. McCloud, call sign "Marshall," went on to become lieutenant general and commander of Alaskan Command, 11th Air Force, and the Alaskan North American Aerospace Defense Command Region, Elmendorf Air Force Base, Alaska. He was killed 26 July 1998 while flying his personally owned YaK-54 aerobatic plane.]

David J. McCloud. *U.S. Air Force*

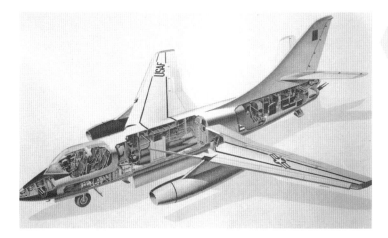

Douglas test pilot George Jansen made a successful first flight of the premier RB-66A Destroyer – Long Beach to Edwards on 28 June 1954. It was powered by two non-afterburning 9,750-pound thrust Allison J751-A-9 turbojet engines with a top speed of 610 miles per hour, with a gross weight of 80,000 pounds. It was 76.2 feet long with a wind span of 72.5 feet. Similar to the USN A3D-1 Skywarrior, which made its first flight as the USAF Tactical Air Command and became known as "Weapon System 308." Although the afore-mentioned premier RB-66A was not designated with an "X" for experimental or "Y" service test, it was nonetheless an X-Plane. *(Douglas Aircraft Company)*

With famed test pilot Alvin M. "Tex" Johnston at the controls, the Boeing Model B-367-80—the "Dash 80," or 707 Jet Stratoliner prototype—made a successful first flight on 15 July 1954, flying to Seattle, Washington, from Renton, where it was built. This was the forerunner to all modern turbojet-powered U.S. jetliners and also served as the prototype of the U.S. Air Force C-135 Stratolifter and KC-135 Stratotanker cargo and tanker aircraft. It also served as an engine test bed but was originally powered by four 10,000-pound-thrust class Pratt & Whitney JT3 turbojet engines, the commercial equivalent of the military J57 series, which gave the U.S. Air Force and U.S. Navy its first supersonic fighters. *Boeing Historical Archives*

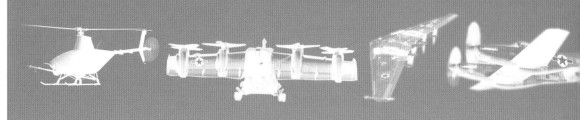

chapter three

THE ROCKET AGE

BY THE BEGINNING OF THE 1940s, primarily due to war in Europe, reaching higher aircraft speeds had become vital—most especially for modern combat aircraft such as fighters. For this was the era when the Jet Age was just dawning, and the fastest piston-powered and propeller-driven aircraft barely surpassed 400 miles per hour.

Unbeknownst to the unsuspecting world at large, Germany was on the fast track to having aircraft speeds in excess of 500 and even 600 miles per hour, with its top-secret jet- and rocket-powered airplane programs. The German aircraft industry first achieved these speeds of more than 100 to 200 miles per hour faster than propeller-driven aircraft with experimental craft, but those speeds were soon surpassed in the worst possible scenario: by other German combat aircraft.

Meanwhile, in both the United States and United Kingdom, even the most generic jet- and rocket-propulsion programs were mostly stagnant. But this all changed when the rest of world got wind of Germany's advanced aircraft jet- and rocket-propulsion systems, and developing such systems became a top priority in both America and Great Britain.

The Rocket Age began in Germany, when on 1 September 1941 the Messerschmitt Me-163A Komet, a small rocket-powered interceptor prototype, made its first successful flight with Rudy Opitz at the controls. In America the Rocket Age began on 5 July 1944, when Northrop test pilot Harry Crosby successfully flew a mockup of what was to be a rocket-powered interceptor pursuit plane known as Model N-12 in the XP-79 program. At the time, however, rocket motor development was less than adequate. So in an attempt to make the XP-79 program successful without rocket propulsion, the one-of-a-kind twin-turbojet-powered XP-79B was built. But on 12 September 1945, on its very first flight at Muroc, it crashed and killed test pilot Harry Crosby. So, as it turned out, U.S. rocket-powered flight had to wait until 1947. And, in an all-out effort to make sure it was successful, a number of dedicated research air vehicles known as X-Planes were built and flown—sometimes with a great deal of success and sometimes with very tragic results.

The Bell X-1 was the first dedicated research airplane in America. Bell Aircraft built three examples, and the first of these rocket-powered X-1s, piloted by U.S. Air Force Captain Charles Yeager, became the first airplane in the world to fly faster than the speed of sound on 14 October 1947 at Muroc Air Force Base. Again with Yeager at the controls, a modified version of the X-1, known as the second generation X-1A, hit Mach 2.44 later—but not before NACA (National Advisory Committee for Aeronautics) test pilot A. Scott Crossfield became the first pilot to fly at twice the speed of sound in the Douglas Skyrocket.

On 14 October 1947 a piloted airplane—the Bell XS-1 (later X-1)—exceeded the speed of sound for the first time. The official transcript of the ground and air communications during that mission follows:

Major Robert L. "Bob" Cardenas (B-29 pilot): Muroc tower, Air Force Eight Zero Zero taxi instructions.

Tower: B-29 Eight Zero Zero cleared runway six. Winds out of east, seven miles an hour.

Cardenas: We cleared to roll?

Tower: Roger, cleared to line up and roll.

Swindell (B-29 flight engineer): She's all yours, major.

Cardenas: All right, Swindell?

Cardenas: Rolling.

B-29 left-side scanner: Left gear full up, left flap full up. One and two [engines] look clean on the takeoff, sir.

B-29 right-side scanner: Right gear full up, right flap full up. Three and four [engines] look good on the takeoff.

Swindell: Roger.

Cardenas: B-29 Eight Zero Zero to Muroc tower. How do you read me, over?

Tower: Loud and clear.

Swindell: Scanners from engineer, 5,000 feet.

Captain Charles E. "Chuck" Yeager (XS-1 pilot): Check list complete, everything OK.

Jack Ridley (XS-1 test pilot and project officer): Roger.

Cardenas: B-29 Eight Zero Zero. Air Force Two Zero One. Hoover, are you guys on the way up?

Robert A. "Bob" Hoover (chase pilot): Yeah, boy.

Cardenas: OK, we're just closing 15.000 feet. About 20 south of the lake [Muroc Dry Lake]. Making a right turn now and heading south.

Hoover: Roger.

Richard "Dick" Frost (Bell engineer): You over El Mirage [Dry Lake], Cardenas?

Cardenas: Coming to the southern end of the lake at 16,000 feet.

Frost: I'll be with you soon.

Hoover: Air Force Two Zero One, where are you B-29?

Cardenas: I am coming around . . .

Hoover: OK, I see you now buddy; coming up to you.

Cardenas: Eight Zero Zero, five-minute warning.

Yeager: OK, Cardenas, loading first stage now. Ridley? Clear to disconnect nitrogen hose and pilot's breathing oxygen?

Ridley: Roger.

Cardenas: Four minutes.

Yeager: Roger, Cardenas; pressurizing fuel tank.

Ridley: Nitrogen hose disconnected. Pilot's breathing oxygen disconnected.

Yeager: Roger, Jack.

NACA Muroc: NACA radar to Air Force Eight Zero Zero, how do you read?

Cardenas: Loud and clear. Three minutes.

Yeager: Pressurizing lox tank. All pressurized.

Frost: Yeager, this is Frost. I'm in position to check your jettison.

Yeager: Roger. Fuel jettison is on.

Frost: Fuel jettison OK.

Yeager: Switch off.

Frost: Shut-off OK.

Cardenas: Two minutes.

Yeager: Lox jettison switch on. Switch off.

Frost: Lox jettison and shut-off are OK.

NACA Muroc: Was that two minutes B-29?

Cardenas: Roger, that was two minutes.

Tower: Muroc Air Force Base to all aircraft. All aircraft stay clear of Muroc Dry Lake area. Test in progress. All aircraft on ground return to parking positions. Repeat: all aircraft stay clear.

Cardenas: B-29 Eight Zero Zero to NACA radar, Muroc Tower, chase aircraft: one minute.

NACA Muroc: NACA radar to Air Force B-29 Eight Zero Zero. You are clear to drop.

Cardenas: Roger.

Ridley: Yeager, this is Ridley. You all set?

Yeager: Hell, yes, let's get it over with.

Ridley: Remember those stabilizer settings.

Yeager: Roger.

Cardenas: Eight Zero Zero. Here is your countdown: 10, 9, 8, 7, 6, 5, 3, 2, 1 – Drop. [Note: Cardenas omitted the number four in the drop count; launch occurred at 10:26 a.m. as the B-29 was flying at 20,000 feet and an indicated airspeed of 250 miles per hour.]

Yeager: Firing four [rocket chamber four] . . . . Four fired. OK . . . will fire two. . . . Two on. . . . Will cut off four. . . . Four off. . . . Will fire three. . . . Three burning now. . . . Will shut off two and fire one. . . . One on. . . . Will fire two again. . . . Two on. . . . Will fire four.

Ridley: How much of a drop [in chamber pressure]?

Yeager: About 40 psi . . . got a rich mixture. . . . Chamber pressures down. . . . Now going up again. . . . Pressures all normal. . . . Will fire three again. . . . Three on . . . acceleration good. . . . Have had mild buffet, usual instability. Say, Ridley, make a note here. Elevator effectiveness regained [as Yeager passed an indicated Mach number of 0.96].

Ridley: Roger. Noted.

Yeager: Ridley! Make another note. There's something wrong with this Mach meter. It's gone screwy!

Ridley: If there is, we'll fix it. Personally, I think you're seeing things.

Yeager: I guess I am, Jack. . . . Will shut down again . . . am shutting off. . . . Shut off. . . . Still going upstairs like a bat. . . . Have jettisoned fuel and lox . . . about 30 percent of each remaining. . . . Still going up . . . have shut off now.

Brigadier General
Robert L. Cardenas.
AFFTC/HO

Brigadier General
Charles E. Yeager.
AFFTC/HO

Jack Ridley
AFFTC/HO

Robert A. Hoover
AFFTC/HO

The Speed of Sound and Mach Numbers

The Mach number (Mn) refers to the method of measuring airspeed that was developed by the Austrian physicist Ernst Mach. It is used to indicate flight velocities in high-speed flight and is related to the speed of sound. The actual speed of sound varies, depending on the altitude above sea level, because sound travels at slightly different speeds at different temperatures, and the temperatures vary according to altitude. At sea level, the speed of sound is about 761 miles per hour (1,225 kilometers per hour). At 20,000 feet (6,096 meters), the speed of sound is 660 mph (1,062 kilometers per hour).

If an aircraft is traveling at one-half the speed of sound, it is said to be traveling at Mach 0.5. A speed of Mach 2 is twice the speed of sound. Because the speed of sound varies, a particular speed at sea level expressed as a Mach number would be faster than the same speed at 30,000 feet (9,144 meters), which would be faster than the same speed at 40,000 feet (12,192 meters). When an aircraft reaches Mach 1, it is said to "break the sound barrier."

The following breakdowns have been generally accepted to classify speeds:

Mach less than 0.8 – subsonic
Mach 0.8 to 1.2 – transonic
Mach 1.2 to 5.0 – supersonic
Mach greater than 5.0 – hypersonic

A "critical Mach number" is the speed of an aircraft (below Mach 1) when the air flowing over some area of the airfoil has reached the speed of sound. For instance, if the air flowing over a wing reaches Mach 1 when the wing is only moving at Mach 0.8, then the wing's critical Mach number is 0.8.

Douglas Aircraft built three D-558-2 Skyrocket aircraft to investigate high-speed flight; that is, supersonic flight in and around Mach 1. But, to everyone's surprise, on 20 November 1953, after being reconfigured for aerial launching and powered with rocket propulsion, a Skyrocket hit an astounding speed of Mach 2.005 (1,291 miles per hour) while passing through 62,000 feet in a dive from 72,000 feet. With this triumph, the U.S. Navy and NACA, now known as NASA, had wrestled the speed mark away from the U.S. Air Force. Then on 12 December that same year, the Air Force's Yeager established a new speed mark with his aforementioned Mach 2.44 blast in the X-1A.

But the world's first trisonic speed flight came at a horrible price, when on 27 September 1956, U.S. Air Force Captain Mel Apt lost control of the Bell X-2 he was flying and the plane crashed, killing him. But just before the X-2 went out of control, because it had an inadequate vertical tail area, it had reached a then unheard of speed of Mach 3.196 (2,094 miles per hour).

Several other second-generation X-1s followed in the form of the X-1B, X-1D, and X-1E. Of these, the X-1E hit a best speed of Mach 2.24 (1,478 miles per hour) on 8 October 1957, with NACA test pilot Joe Walker at the helm. Then, on a later flight, again with Walker in control, the X-1E hit a best altitude of 73,000 feet (13.8 miles).

However, it was not until the advent of the North American X-15 that trisonic and hyper-sonic flight became commonplace. These three planes flew a total of 199 flights, in which they established a best speed of Mach 6.70 (4,520 miles per hour) and a best altitude of 354,200 feet (67.08 miles). The pilots who accomplished these feats on 22 August 1963 and on 3 October 1967 were NASA pilot Joe Walker and U.S. Air Force Major William Knight, respectively.

Two Chance Vought XF8U-1 Crusader aircraft were built and thoroughly tested. The U.S. Navy was more than pleased with their performance and ordered production F8U-1s (later F-8As) as carrier-borne fleet point- and area-defense fighter-interceptor aircraft. The first of two XF8U-1 airplanes, known as One-X, made a successful first flight at Edwards AFB on 25 March 1955 with Chance Vought test pilot John Konrad at the controls. It exceeded Mach 1 in level-attitude flight at 30,000 feet during its first flight, becoming the first U.S. Navy supersonic fighter. Both examples were powered by single afterburning 15,000-pound-thrust class Pratt & Whitney J57-P-11 Turbo Wasp turbojet engines. The XF8U-1s measured 54.25 feet in length, 15.75 feet in height, with wingspans of 35.67 feet; maximum weight was 27,000 pounds. In combat during the Vietnam War, the Crusader outperformed all other American fighters, downing 19 MiG-17 and MiG-21 aircraft. *Vought Heritage*

Powered by four afterburning 13,000-pound-thrust Allison J71-A-4 turbojet engines, the first of two Martin XP6M-1 SeaMaster airplanes made its first flight on 14 July 1955 with Martin test pilot George Rodney in command. Martin built two XP6M-1s, six service test YP6M-1s and eight production P6M-2s before the SeaMaster program was canceled on 21 August 1959 due to, according to the U.S. Navy, "unforeseen technical difficulties." The eight production P6M-2 airplanes were powered by four afterburning 15,800-pound-thrust Pratt & Whitney J75-P-2 turbojet engines, and they had a maximum speed of 686 miles per hour (with a limiting Mach of .95). They were 134 feet 0.5 inches long, 32 feet 4.675 inches high and had a wingspan of 102 feet 10.55 inches; gross weight was 195,000 pounds. The first XP6M-1 is shown during its secret roll-out on 21 December 1954; the SeaMaster program was not announced publicly until November 1955, when the second XP6M-1 was ceremoniously rolled out. The first SeaMaster and its four-man crew were lost in a mysterious crash into Chesapeake Bay on 7 December 1955. The fault of the crash remains unknown. *Martin Museum via Stan Piet*

Flown primarily by Grumman test pilot Corwin Meyer, the Grumman F11F-1F Super Tiger was developed to compete with the doublesonic Lockheed F-104 Starfighter. The Super Tiger made its first flight at Edwards AFB on 25 May 1956 with Meyer at the controls. While its performance was admirable, it was eventually abandoned in favor of the F-104, which already had some two years advantage over the Super Tiger in its overall development. The F11F-1F does, however, retain the distinction of being the first doublesonic fighter to fly in U.S. Navy colors. The F11F-1F Super Tiger was powered by a single afterburning 15,000–pound-thrust General Electric J79-GE-3 turbojet engine. It reached its maximum speed of Mach 2.04 on 2 May 1957. It is 40 feet 10 inches long, 14 feet 4.75 inches high, and had a wingspan of 31 feet 7.5 inches; gross weight was 26,000 pounds. *AFFTC/HO*

Republic test pilot Russell Roth was the pilot when the first of two YF-105A Thunderchief aircraft made its first flight at Edwards AFB on 22 October 1955. The two YF-105As were powered by single afterburning 15,000-pound-thrust Pratt & Whitney J57-P-25 turbojet engines as an interim measure. Four YF-105Bs followed with afterburning 24,500-pound-thrust Pratt & Whitney J75-P-3 turbojet engines, which increased top speed from Mach 1.2 to Mach 2.3. The YF-105A was 61 feet 5 inches long, 17 feet 6 inches high and had a wingspan of 34 feet 9 inches. The F-105 competed against the North American F-107 in the U.S. Air Force's advanced tactical fighter-bomber program of the late 1950s, which the F-105 ultimately won. Good as the F-107 was, it could not match the Thunderchief's headstart (the F-105 flew some 11 months before the F-107) and its awesome load-carrying ability. Production F-105s were nuclear capable, and they could carry a single MK28, MK57 or MK61 nuclear bomb within their internal weapons bays. Following in the footsteps of the F-84 series of fighters, the F-105 Thunderchief was the last fighter produced by the Republic Aircraft Corporation. Shown is the No. 2 YF-105A (above) during a "buddy system" inflight refueling test with the third YF-105B. *AFFTC/HO*

Piloted by Convair test pilot Beryl Erickson, the Convair (later General Dynamics) YB-58 Hustler made a successful first flight on 11 November 1956. It was flown from and back to the Fort Worth division of Convair at Carswell AFB, Texas; its second flight of about one hour followed on 14 November. Powered by four afterburning 15,000–pound-thrust-class GE J79 turbojet engines, this delta-winged beauty was the world's first supersonic strategic bomber, with a top speed of Mach 1.55 at its combat weight of 82,600 pounds. Flying clean however, its top speed was nearly Mach 2 at 1.75 (1,300 miles per hour). The U.S. Air Force eventually bought 116 Hustlers, including the 30 early production ones, which served as prototypes and service test aircraft. Most of them were brought up to production standard after their respective evaluation programs had been completed. *AFFTC/HO*

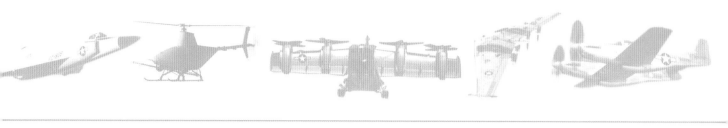

The first of three service test North American F-107A airplanes made its first flight at Edwards AFB on 10 September 1956 with NAA test pilot Robert Baker under the canopy. Unofficially dubbed Ultra Sabre due to its advanced features over its F-86 Sabre and F-100 Super Sabre predecessors, the trio of F-107A aircraft flew a total of 272 times over 176 hours, 30 minutes. The three P&W J75-powered airplanes, U.S. Air Force serial numbers 55-5118, -5119 and -5120, respectively flew 93, 61, and 118 times over several years. The Mach 2.2-plus F-107A was in competition with the Republic YF-105B Thunderchief—a competition it eventually lost. NASA, however, flew the F-107As a number of additional times at Edwards AFB after North American and the U.S. Air Force were through with them, continuing its research into the aeronautical sciences. *North American Aviation via Gene Boswell*

Convair test pilot Richard Johnson was at the controls of the premier YF-106A Delta Dart when it made its first flight at Edwards AFB on 26 December 1956. And during this first test flight, Johnson romped to a speed of Mach 1.9 at 57,000 feet! Two YF-106As were built with single afterburning 24,500-pound-thrust Pratt & Whitney J75-P-17 turbojet engines, which gave them a maximum speed of Mach 2.3. The YF-106A Delta Dart is 70 feet 8.75 inches long, 20 feet 3.33 inches high with a delta-shaped wingspan of 38 feet 1 inch; gross weight was 35,000 pounds. Originally known as the YF-102B, the YF-106A became Weapon System 201B and led to the production of 340 F-106As and F-106Bs. Not only was the F-106 a good-looking airplane; it is regarded as being the best operational interceptor ever built. *AFFTC/HO*

Chance Vought test pilot John Konrad made a successful first flight of the Chance Vought XF8U-3 Crusader III (or Super Crusader) at Edwards AFB on 3 June 1958. It was powered by a single afterburning 29,500-pound-thrust Pratt & Whitney J75-P-5A turbojet engine which gave it a top speed of Mach 2.39 (1,600 miles per hour). It is 58.67 feet long, 16.34 feet high with a wingspan of 38.92 feet; gross weight was 37,860 pounds. Three XF8U-3s were built and flown in a competition with the McDonnell XF4H-1 Phantom II, which was ultimately preferred over the Super Crusader because of its two-man-crew, two-engine configuration. One projected version of the Crusader II was to feature the use of a single afterburning 34,000-pound-thrust class Pratt & Whitney J58 turbojet engine for triplesonic speed, but that version was not built. *LTV*

Northrop test pilot Lewis Nelson made the first flight of the premier Northrop Model N-156F Freedom Fighter on 30 July 1959 at Edwards AFB. It was powered by two afterburning 4,080-pound-thrust General Electric J85-GE-13 turbojet engines; top speed was Mach 1.3. Three were built, and they were later redesignated YF-5A. The YF-5A is 47 feet 2 inches long, 13 feet 2 inches high with a wingspan of 25 feet 10 inches; gross weight was 13,430 pounds. The success of the YF-5As led to production of numerous F-5A/B Freedom Fighter and follow-on F-5E/F Tiger II lightweight fighter aircraft. An advanced version of the Tiger II, at first designated F-5G, ultimately became the F-20 Tigershark. *AFFTC/HO*

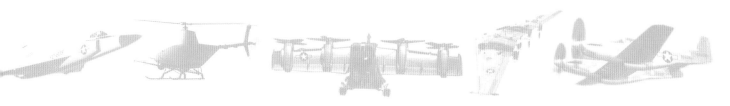

On 12 January 1962 two McDonnell F4H-1F Phantom II aircraft arrived at Langley AFB, Virginia, to be evaluated by the Tactical Air Command (TAC) of the U.S. Air Force. The air force had already made it clear that it wanted this U.S. Navy fighter in its stable and quickly redesignated it YF-110A and renamed it Spectre. Another 27 F4H-1Fs followed for the U.S. Air Force/TAC evaluation program. The U.S. Air Force quickly adopted the type and set wheels in motion to procure a number of production F-110As. But in September 1962 the Department of Defense put forth a new aircraft designation system, and the F4H-1F became the F-4B. Since the F-110A would be the next production version of the U.S. Navy Phantom II, by Department of Defense order, it was redesignated F-4C. So the first two YF-110As became YF-4Cs, and the remaining 27 F-4Bs were returned to the U.S. Navy. Furthermore, the name Spectre was abolished and the U.S. Air Force was forced to use the name Phantom II. So on 27 May 1963, with McDonnell test pilot Bob Little in the seat, the first production F-4C Phantom II made a successful first flight at St. Louis, Missouri. The YF-4C was 58 feet 3.13 inches long, 16 feet 3 inches high with a wingspan of 34 feet 4.88 inches. It was powered by two augmented 17,000-pound-thrust General Electric J79-GE-15 turbojet engines; maximum speed was Mach 2.3-plus. *AFFTC/HO*

On 17 December 1963 the premier Lockheed YC-141A Starlifter made a successful first flight at Marietta, Georgia. The T-tailed production C-141A is powered by four nonafterburning 21,000-pound-thrust Pratt & Whitney TF33-P-7 turbofan-jet engines, which provide a top speed of 560 miles per hour. It is 145 feet 0 inches long, 39 feet 4 inches high with a wingspan of 160 feet 0 inches; gross weight is about 323,000 pounds. Redesignated C-141A after testing, the flight test success of the premier Starlifter led to the production of numerous C-141As. Most of these were later modified with stretched fuselages, new wings, and in-flight refueling capability and subsequently redesignated C-141B. Only now are some C-141Bs being retired as more and more Boeing C-17As become operational.

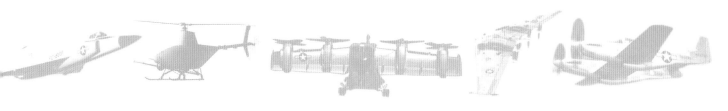

Ling-Temco-Vought test pilot John Konrad made the maiden flight of the premier LTV YA-7A Corsair II on 27 September 1965 at Dallas, Texas. It was powered by a single nonaugmented 11,300-pound-thrust class Pratt & Whitney TF30-P-6 turbofan-jet engine, which gave it a top speed of 680 miles per hour. It is 46 feet 1 inch long, 16 feet 0 inches high with a shoulder-mounted wingspan of 38 feet 9 inches; gross weight was about 30,000 pounds. An A-7D version was developed for the U.S. Air Force. The U.S. Navy A-7 Corsair II fleet was an attack-type, carrier-borne aircraft workhorse for that service; it served well indeed in the Vietnam War. *LTV*

The first of two North American Aviation XB-70A Valkyrie aircraft made a successful first flight from Palmdale to Edwards AFB on 21 September 1964 with North American test pilot Al White in the left seat and U.S. Air Force Colonel Joe Cotton in the right seat. Originally designed to replace the subsonic Boeing B-52 Stratofortress, this triplesonic (2,000 miles per hour) strategic bombardment type of air vehicle was instead used to investigate aerodynamic phenomenon such as sonic booms. Booms would be created by large and heavy aircraft such as the upcoming Supersonic Transport (SST) aircraft like the projected Boeing 2707 (canceled 24 March 1971), the British/French Concorde, and the Russian Tupolev Tu-144, which were both built. Since the Valkyrie was canceled as a weapon system, only one other example was built; first flown on 17 July 1965, it, too, was used only for research. These aircraft were large and heavy, measuring 185feet in length, 30 feet in height, and with wingspan of 105 feet. Their maximum takeoff weight was more than 500,000 pounds. They were each powered by six 30,000-pound-thrust class GE YJ93-GE-3 afterburning turbojet engines, and each one of these aircraft exceeded Mach 3 (Mach 3.07 best) and 70,000 feet (74,000 feet best) during their respective North American Aviation /U.S. Air Force/NASA flight test programs. The second example was lost in a midair collision with a NASA F-104 on 6 June 1966, which killed NASA test pilot Joe Walker and U.S. Air Force test pilot Major Carl Cross. The first example, flown from Edwards AFB to the U.S. Air Force Museum at Dayton, Ohio, on 4 February 1969, remains on display. *NASA*

Derived from the earlier F-8 Crusader and the A-7 itself, a proposed version known as the A-7F was to have been supersonic and, in essence, a rebirth of the Crusader. Two Ling-Temco-Vought YA-7Fs were built and flown, and the first example flew on 29 November 1989 with LTV test pilot Jim Read in control. The first of the two YA-7Fs is shown in this photograph. *LTV*

Developed under the U.S. Air Force Cargo Experimental-Heavy Logistics System (CX-HLS) program, the premier Lockheed C-5A Galaxy made its successful first flight at Marietta, Georgia, on 30 June 1968. It was powered by four nonaugmented 41,000-pound-thrust General Electric TF39-GE-1 turbofan-jet engines, which gave it a top speed of 570 miles per hour. It is 247 feet 9 1/2 inches long, 65 feet 1 1/4 inches high, with a wingspan of 222 feet 8 1/2 inches; gross weight was 837,000 pounds. The C-5 remains the largest and heaviest transport in U.S. Air Force inventory and one of the world's biggest aircraft. Although the first C-5A was not designated XC-5A or YC-5A, it still served as a dedicated prototype airplane. *AFFTC/HO*

The first of eight YA-3A Viking service test aircraft made its first flight at Palmdale on 21 January 1972, manned by Lockheed test pilot John Christiansen and copilot Lyle Schaefer. The YS-3A is 53 feet 4 inches long, 22 feet 9 inches high, with a wingspan of 68 feet 8 inches; gross weight was 43,000 pounds. It was powered by two nonafterburning 9,275-pound-thrust General Electric TF34-GE-2 turbofan-jet engines. Its top speed was about 550 miles per hour. In a bit of a rarity, the YA-3A was developed without any competing aircraft to endanger its survival. But it did all it was expected to do, went into full-scale production, and is still operational today. Production carrier-based S-3 Vikings are used for a number of missions, including submarine hunter/killer, mine laying, and electronic warfare. *Lockheed Martin*

The first of two Fairchild Republic (formerly Republic Aircraft) YA-10A Thunderbolt II airplanes made a successful first flight at Edwards AFB with Republic test pilot Howard Nelson at the controls. The YA-10A, as well as the Northrop YA-9A, competed in the U.S. Air Force A-X (Attack-Experimental) program whereby the winner would serve as a production close air support aircraft for the Tactical Air Command of the U.S. Air Force. The service test YA-10A is 53 feet 4 inches long, 17 feet 8 inches high with a wingspan of 57 feet 6 inches; gross weight was 47,000 pounds. It was powered by two nonafterburning 9,000-pound-thrust General Electric TF34-GE-100 turbofan-jet engines which gave it a maximum subsonic speed of 450 miles per hour. So successful was the YA-10A flight test program, it went on to win the A-X competition. *AFFTC/HO*

Northrop built two YA-9A close air support demonstrators, and the first example, piloted by Northrop test pilot Lewis Nelson (no relation to Howard Nelson), made a successful first flight at Edwards AFB on 30 May 1972. TheYA-9A was 53 feet 6 inches long, 16 feet 11 inches high, with a wingspan of 58 feet 0 inches. Gross weight was 42,000 pounds. It was powered by two nonaugmented 7,500-pound-thrust Lycoming F102-LD-100 turbofan-jet engines, which gave it a top speed of 450 miles per hour. The YA-9A flight test program was nearly flawless. However, the U.S. Air Force judged the YA-10A as best overall, and it won the A-X competition. The No. 1 YA-9A service test airplane now resides at the Air Force Flight Test Center Museum at Edwards AFB, while the No. 2 is on display at the March Field Museum. *AFFTC/HO*

Still the world's premier air superiority fighter—that is, until the F/A-22 air dominance fighter comes on line in 2005—the first McDonnell Douglas YF-15A Eagle made its first flight at Edwards on 27 July 1972 with McDonnell Douglas test pilot Irving Burrows at the helm. In all, 20 full-scale development (FSD) single-seat F-15A and tandem-seat F-15B (formerly TF-15A) airplanes were evaluated at Edwards AFB. The YF-15A is 63 feet 9.75 inches long and 18 feet 7.5 inches high, with a wingspan of 42 feet 9.75 inches. It was powered by two augmented 25,000-pound-thrust Pratt & Whitney F100-PW-100 turbofan engines, which gave it a Mach 2.5-plus top speed and a whopping 40,000 feet-per-minute climb rate. *AFFTC/HO*

During the time period of 16 January to 1 February 1975, one of the 20 FSD McDonnell Douglas F-15A Eagle airplanes, named *Streak Eagle*, was modified to perform all-out time-to-climb evaluations, known as Project Streak Eagle, at Grand Forks AFB, North Dakota. Three U.S. Air Force pilots subsequently established eight officially recognized time-to-climb records during that two-week period. One of these marks, a climb to 98,425.19 feet (30,000 meters) in just 3.463 minutes (207.80 seconds) was achieved on 1 February 1975, the final day. This mark has not yet been broken by any other American fighter. But most likely, in the near future the U.S. Air Force may demonstrate the maximum climb capabilities of its new F/A-22 Raptor, which by a slight stretch of the imagination could easily exceed the marks established by the *Streak Eagle*. *U.S. Air Force*

The B-1B is a highly modified version of the canceled B-1A and the first of 100 Rockwell (now Boeing North American) B-1B Lancer bombers. The B-1B made its first flight on 18 October 1984 from Palmdale to Edwards AFB, 3 hours and 20 minutes. It was piloted by Rockwell test pilot M. L. Evenson and copiloted by U.S. Air Force Lieutenant Colonel Leroy Schroeder. The Lancer is 143 feet 3.5 inches long, 33 feet 7.25 inches high and has a wingspan of 136 feet 8.5 inches fully extended (78 feet 2.5 inches fully swept aft); gross weight is 477,000 pounds. The B-1B is powered by four augmented 30,780-pound-thrust General Electric F101-GE-102 turbofan jet engines which give it a top speed of Mach 1.25. The B-1B features a variable-geometry swing-wing configuration and reduced radar cross-section. *U.S. Air Force*

Grumman (now Northrop Grumman) built two X-29A airplanes to demonstrate high-speed flight with a forward swept wing (FSW) configuration. Grumman test pilot Charles Sewell made the first successful test flight of the No. 1 X-29A at Edwards AFB on 14 December 1984. The X-29A is 48 feet long, 14 feet high with a wingspan of 27 feet; gross weight was 17,600 pounds. Both X-29A airplanes were powered by single 16,000-pound-thrust General Electric F404-GE-400 turbofan jet engines, and during one flight, an X-29A hit Mach 1.23 (830 miles per hour) – the fastest speed ever flown by an FSW-configured aircraft. As one of the most successful test flight programs ever flown at Edwards, the two X-29As flew a total of 242 flights in 178.5 flying hours. *Northrop Grumman*

A General Dynamics F-111A – formerly the F-111 transonic aircraft technology (TACT) and the F-111 advanced fighter technology integration (AFTI) aircraft, was modified by Boeing to incorporate a wing that allowed the curvature of the leading and trailing edges to be varied in flight. This F-111 mission adaptive wing (MAW) airplane was built to fly with optimum wing curvatures for subsonic, transonic, and supersonic speeds to investigate the potential for greater flight efficiency. The F-111 MAW airplane made the first of its 59 total flights on 18 October 1985. It was a very successful flight test program, and the NASA F/A-18 AAW program of today (which see later in text) is a result of the successful F-111 MAW program. All in all, four NASA and six U.S. Air Force pilots flew the F-111 MAW before program's end on 22 December 1988, for a total of 144.9 flying hours. *NASA*

The premier Boeing (formerly McDonnell Douglas) F-15E Strike Eagle made its first flight at St. Louis, Missouri, on 11 December 1986 with company test pilot Gary Jennings in command. Larger and heavier than the B-25 Mitchell medium class bomber of World War II fame, the F-15E Strike Eagle is 63.8 feet long, 18.5 feet high with a wingspan of 42.8 feet; gross weight is 81,000 pounds. It is powered by two afterburning 25,000 or 29,000-pound-thrust Pratt & Whitney F100-PW-220 or F100-PW-229 turbofan-jet engines, which give it a top speed of Mach 2.5-plus. As a very large fighter-bomber, the F-15E can carry a tremendous amount of ordnance. Having first earned its combat spurs in Operation Desert Storm, the F-15E is still in production. *Boeing*

The premier McDonnell Douglas C-17A Globemaster III made a successful first flight from Long Beach, California, to Edwards AFB on 15 September 1991 with McDonnell Douglas test pilot Bill Casey in command. The C-17A is 174 feet long, 55 feet 1 inch high, and has a wingspan of 169 feet 8 inches. It is powered by four nonaugmented 40,440-pound-thrust Pratt & Whitney F117-PW-100 turbofan engines, which give it a normal cruise speed of Mach 0.77 (508.2 miles per hour). It was developed as a large cargo transport aircraft to carry outsized equipment, such as the massive M1A1/A2 Abrams main battle tank. *AFFTC/HO*

Bell Aircraft built three X-1 (formerly XS-1) airplanes for the purpose of flying beyond the speed of sound. Bell test pilot Chalmers Goodlin made the first powered flight of an X-1 on 9 December 1946 at Muroc AAB, but then on 14 October 1947, U.S. Air Force Capt. Chuck Yeager took the X-1 to the speed for which it was designed when he exceeded Mach 1(actually Mach 1.06 at 43,000 feet). He therefore became the first human on the planet to travel faster than the speed of sound (approximately 1,100 feet per second, or 750 miles per hour). The X-1 was 30 feet 11 inches long, 10 feet 10 inches high, with a wingspan of 28 feet; gross weight was 12,250 pounds. It was powered by a single four-chamber 6,000-pound-thrust Reaction Motors XLR11-RM-3 rocket motor. It ultimately reached a maximum altitude of 71,900 feet and a maximum speed of Mach 1.45 (957 miles per hour). These three first-generation X-1 airplanes led to the creation of four second-generation X-1s respectively designated X-1A, X-1B, X-1D and X-1E. *NASA*

Three Douglas D-558-2 Skyrocket aircraft were built for the U.S. Navy to investigate the transonic speed regime, with hope of exceeding the speed of sound with sweptback flying surfaces. The first example, flown by Douglas test pilot John Martin, made its first flight at Muroc on 4 February 1948. The D-558-2 was 42 feet long, 12 feet 8 inches high with a wingspan of 25 feet; gross weight was 15,260 pounds. The original Skyrocket was powered by a single nonafterburning 3,000-pound-thrust-class Westinghouse J34-WE-40 turbojet engine. The later, modified Skyrocket was powered by a single four-chamber 6,000-pound-thrust Reaction Motors XLR8-RM-5 (or -6) rocket motor which, after being air-dropped by a mother plane, allowed it to achieve a maximum speed of Mach 2.005 (1,325 miles per hour) and a maximum altitude of 83,235 feet. It therefore became the first airplane in the world to fly at doublesonic speed. There was to be a third version of the D-558 family originally known as the D-558-3, which became the proposed but not produced Mach 7-plus Model D-684 Skyflash. *NASA*

Two swept-wing Bell X-2 aircraft were built to investigate speeds nearing and/or exceeding Mach 2. However, on 27 September 1956, with U.S. Air Force test pilot Captain Mel Apt at the controls, it became the first plane in the world to exceed Mach 3, hitting Mach 3.2 (2,094 miles per hour). Most unfortunately, the airplane went out of control during that flight, and Apt, the first human to exceed 2,000 miles per hour, was killed. This accident was the result of a newly discovered aerodynamic phenomenon known as "inertia coupling," instability caused by the lack of adequate vertical tail area on high-speed aircraft. Twenty days earlier, with U.S. Air Force test pilot Capt. Iven C. Kincheloe Jr. at the controls, the same airplane, X-2 No. 1, had hit a peak altitude of 126,200 feet—the highest ever flown at the time. The air-launched X-2 aircraft were 37 feet 10 inches long, with a wingspan of 32 feet 3 inches; empty weight was 12,400 pounds. They were both powered by a single 15,000-pound static-thrust throttleable Curtiss-Wright XLR25 rocket motor. Unfortunately, X-2 No. 2 was lost on 12 May 1953 before it could ever make any of its test flights. As it happened, while aloft in the belly of its Boeing B-50 mother plane during captive carry tests, there was an explosion and the X-2 had to be ejected to save the crew members on the mother plane. It subsequently fell into Lake Ontario near Buffalo, New York, where it remains today. *NASA*

The first powered flight of the second-generation X-1, the Bell X-1A, was made at Edwards on 21 February 1953. Then, on 12 December 1953, with U.S. Air Force Major Chuck Yeager at the controls, the X-1A roared to a top speed of Mach 2.44 (1,650 miles per hour), breaking the previous mark of Mach 2.005 set by a Douglas D-558-2 Skyrocket. The X-1A was powered by a single four-chamber 6,000-pound-thrust Reaction Motors XLR11-RM-5 rocket motor. It was 35 feet 8 inches long and had a wingspan of 28 feet 0 inches; launch weight was 16,490 pounds. The X-1A ultimately achieved a record maximum altitude of 90,400 feet on 26 August 1954 with U.S. Air Force Major Arthur Murray at the controls. *NASA*

The Chance Vought XSSM-N-9 Regulus II was an advanced supersonic cruise missile based on the earlier Regulus I, and its first test flight was successfully accomplished on 29 May 1956 at Edwards AFB. It was powered by a single 14,600-pound-thrust J65-W-6 turbojet engine, which gave it a top speed of Mach 1.8. However, the production Regulus II was powered by a single 15,600-pound-thrust General Electric J79-GE-3 turbojet engine; top speed was Mach 2. The Regulus II was 57.5 feet long and 15.67 feet high, with a wingspan of 20.08 feet; gross weight was 16,000 pounds. The production SSM-N-9 (redesignated RGM-15A) carried a nuclear warhead and was launched from submarines. *AFFTC/HO*

The first powered flight of the North American X-15 was achieved on 17 September 1959 with North American test pilot Scott Crossfield at the controls. Three X-15s were built, and they measure 49 feet 2 inches long, 13 feet 1 inch high (with lower ventral stabilizer), and have a wingspan of 22 feet 4 inches. The X-15 was originally powered by a single 50,000-pound-thrust Reaction Motors XLR99 rocket motor, which made it the world's first air vehicle to reach Mach numbers of 4, 5 and then 6 and a maximum altitude of 354,200 feet (67.08 miles). The highly modified X-15A-2, with a 57,000-pound-thrust XLR99-RM-2 rocket motor, reached a maximum speed of Mach 6.70 (4,520 miles per hour). The X-15A-2 made its first flight on 25 June 1964, piloted by U.S. Air Force test pilot Major Robert Rushworth. *NASA*

NASA pilot Neil A. Armstrong checks out the propulsive system of the first of two Bell-built lunar landing research vehicles (LLRV) at the Dryden Flight Research Center facility at Edwards AFB on 30 October 1964. The two LLRVs were tested from 1964 to 1966 to develop a piloting and procedures program to train Apollo astronauts for lunar landings and takeoffs. These craft were flown to study controls, pilot displays, visibility, propulsion control, and flight dynamics on a vehicle that could simulate flight in an Apollo lunar module. Its propulsion system was a single 4,200-pound-thrust turbofan-jet engine with a gimbaling engine exhaust nozzle for vehicle control. Additional vehicle control came from a series of hydrogen peroxide rockets. It was these two odd-looking LLRVs that helped make all six moon landings and takeoffs the successes they were. *NASA*

On 12 April 1981 the space shuttle orbiter *Columbia* blasted off into orbit from Pad 39A at Kennedy Space Center on the STS-1 (space transportation system-1) mission. It was manned by pilot Robert Crippen and mission commander John Young. Two days later, on 14 April, as had been preplanned, *Columbia* made a successful airplanelike landing at Edwards AFB. The space shuttle is 184.2 feet long and 56.67 feet high, with a wingspan of 78.06 feet; empty weight is about 242,000 pounds. On ascent, space shuttles have three Boeing-Rocketdyne liquid-fueled main engines with variable thrust. Each one can generate 418,660 pounds of thrust at sea level (maximum: 109 percent power level). Four test flights, as it were—STS-1 through STS-4—proved the space shuttle worthy of continued orbital flights, and numerous operational flights have been made since. However, two catastrophic accidents have marred the otherwise excellent record of the space shuttle: On 28 January 1986 the space shuttle *Challenger* was lost during ascent, killing all of her crew, and on 1 February 2003 the space shuttle *Columbia* and her seven crew members were lost during a reentry malfunction. *NASA*

chapter four

STRANGE SHAPES

DURING THE 1970s, a number of strange shapes appeared in the skies above Edwards Air Force Base. These wingless, wedge-shaped air vehicles were called lifting bodies and their successes and failures eventually allowed America to build and fly its fleet of space shuttles. These lifting bodies included the unpowered M2-F1 "flying bathtub" and the powered M2-F2, M2-F3, Martin X-23 PRIME, Martin X-24A, and X-24B, and the Northrop HL-10 and HL-20.

On 18 February 1970, the air-launched Northrop HL-10 hit Mach 1.86 (1,200 miles per hour), which turned out to be the highest speed ever attained by a lifting-body air vehicle. A U.S. Air Force test pilot, Major Pete Hoag, flew the craft. Nine days later, on 27 February, NASA test pilot Bill Dana flew the HL-10 to 90,303 feet, the highest altitude ever reached by a lifting body.

These amazing vehicles were forerunners of the space shuttle, which is capable of at least 350 mile-high orbits above Earth while traveling at 17,500 miles per hour. The shuttles were made possible in part by the many years of scientific research into rocket-powered flight. That research began in earnest with the Bell X-1 in December 1946 and led through development of the North American X-15A-2 in October 1968; the fleet of lifting bodies, such as the Martin X-24B and Northrop HL-10; and, of course, the multitude of rocket-powered ballistic missiles like the General Dynamics (Convair) HGM-16 Atlas and Boeing LGM-30 Minuteman. Since the first space shuttle mission in April 1981, now more than 22 years ago, more than 100 follow-on missions have been flown by these relatively large aerospace vehicles, each roughly the size of a Boeing Model B-717 100-passenger jetliner.

Prior to the NASA space shuttles, as far as speed and altitude goes, NASA's Saturn V moon rockets propelled astronauts into space. During six successful missions from July 1969 through December 1972, the Saturn Vs took 12 astronauts to the surface of the Moon in their lunar modules and returned them safely to Earth in their Apollo space capsules.

On 10 December 1955 Ryan test pilot Pete Girard made a conventional first flight of the first of two jet-powered X-13 vertical takeoff and landing (VTOL) air vehicles at Edwards AFB. But it did not complete its first full VTOL demonstration flight until 11 April 1957, when it took-off vertically, transitioned to conventional flight, and then landed vertically. The second example made its first flight on 28 May 1956. The X-13 Vertijet was powered by a single nonafterburning 10,000-pound-thrust Rolls-Royce Avon turbojet engine. It is 23 feet 5 inches long, 15 feet 2 inches high and it has a wingspan of 21 feet 0 inches; gross weight was 7,200 pounds. Although the Ryan X-13 Vertijet accomplished all it was asked to do, the British AV-8 Harrier would one day be more appealing to the U.S. armed forces, and an operational version of the X-13 was not forthcoming. The second X-13 went to the Air Force Museum in 1959, while the first X-13 went to the Smithsonian Institution in 1960. *AFFTC/HO*

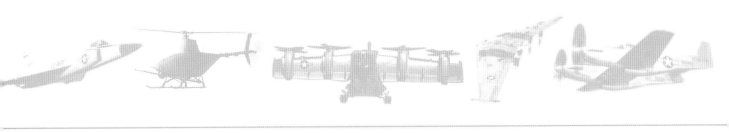

Ling-Temco-Vought (LTV) built five XC-142A tilt-wing vertical/short takeoff and landing (V/STOL) air vehicles that were extensively flight tested by the U.S. Air Force, U.S. Army, U.S. Navy, and NASA for a number of years. The first example made a successful first flight at Dallas, Texas, on 26 September 1964 with LTV test pilot John Konrad at the controls. On 11 January 1965 it made its first transitional flight, in which it took-off vertically, converted to forward flight and then landed vertically. The XC-142A was powered by four 3,080-horsepower General Electric T64 turboprop-jet engines, which gave it a top speed of 400 miles per hour. It is 58 feet 2 inches long, 25 feet 0 inches high with a wingspan of 67 feet 6 inches; gross weight was 41,500 pounds. Only one example of the XC-142A remains, and it is on display at the Air Force Museum in Dayton, Ohio; it was flown to that location in 1970. *LTV*

Northrop built one HL-10 (horizontal lander, model No. 10) lifting body, and its first powered flight at Edwards AFB was on 13 November 1968, with NASA test pilot Bruce Peterson at the controls. U.S. Air Force test pilot Peter Hoag flew it to it fastest speed of Mach 1.86 (1,228 miles per hour) on 18 February 1970 while NASA test pilot Bill Dana took it to its highest altitude of 90,030 feet nine days later on 27 February. The HL-10 is 22 feet 2 inches long, 11 feet 5 inches high, and 15 feet 7 inches wide at its widest point; gross weight was 9,000 pounds. It was powered by a single four-chamber 8,000-pound-thrust Reaction Motors XLR11 rocket motor. The Northrop HL-10 program was initiated as a natural follow-on lifting body demonstrator to the M2-F1, M2-F2, and M2-F3 lifting body flight test programs. *NASA*

Martin Marietta built one X-24B lifting body; its first powered flight was on 15 November 1973 at Edwards AFB, with NASA pilot John Manke was at the controls. The X-24B was powered by a single four-chamber 8,000-pound-thrust Reaction Motors XLR11-RM-13 rocket motor, which ultimately gave it a top speed of 1,163 miles per hour (Mach 1.76) at 74,130 feet. The X-24B is 37 feet 6 inches long and 10 feet 4 inches high, with a maximum width of 19 feet 2 inches; gross weight was 13,000 pounds. It made its last of 36 flights on 9 September 1975. If not for the great success of the lifting body program, the space shuttle program might never have evolved. The X-24B was not the fastest of all of the lifting bodies that were built and flown, but it was the second-fastest. *NASA*

Martin Marietta built one X-24A lifting body, and its first unpowered glide flight came about on 17 April 1969. The first powered flight of the X-24A was successfully completed at Edwards AFB on 19 March 1970, with NASA pilot Jarauld Gentry in command. The wedge-shaped X-24A was 24 feet 6 inches long and 10 feet 4 inches high, with a maximum width of 13 feet 8 inches; gross weight was 10,700 pounds. It was powered by a single four-chamber 8,000-pound-thrust Reaction Motors XLR11-RM-13 rocket motor, which took it to a maximum speed of 1,036 miles per hour (Mach 1.6) at 71,407 feet. The X-24A made 28 flights, the last of which occurred on 4 June 1971. The X-24A, also known as the SV-5P, was later rebuilt to serve as the X-24B. *NASA*

Developed as a lightweight fighter (LWF), two General Dynamics YF-16s were produced to demonstrate this specific quality. The first example made an unexpected first flight at Edwards AFB on 21 January 1974 during a high-speed taxi test. Again with General Dynamics' test pilot Phillip Oestricher at the controls, the official first flight came about on 2 February 1974. The second YF-16 made its first flight on 9 March 1974 with General Dynamics test pilot Neil Anderson in command. After the fly-off against the Northrop YF-17, the YF-16 emerged as winner of the LWF competition. Both of the YF-16s were powered by single augmented 23,800-pound-thrust Pratt & Whitney F100-PW-200 turbofan engines, which offered Mach 2-plus speed. And as a LWF the YF-16 and subsequent F-16s were/are capable of 9g maneuvers. In addition to the U.S. Air Force, U.S. allies and friends widely use the F-16. The YF-16 is 46 feet 6 inches long, 16 feet 3 inches high, and has a wingspan of 31 feet; gross weight was 27,000 pounds. The LWF program metamorphosed into the air combat fighter (ACF) program and likewise pitted the YF-16s against the YF-17s. It was announced on 13 January 1975 that the YF-16 had won the combined LWF/ACF competitions. The F-16 wasn't officially named Fighting Falcon until it became operational. *AFFTC/HO*

The first of two Northrop YF-17s made its first flight at Edwards on 9 June 1974, three full months after the second YF-16 had first taken wing. It was controlled by Northrop test Henry Chouteau. A few days later Chouteau exceeded the speed of sound in level flight at 30,000 feet without the use of augmentation, which was a first in aviation. The second YF-17 Cobra (unofficial name) made its first flight on 21 August 1974. The YF-17 is 56 feet long, 14 feet 6 inches high with a 35 feet wingspan; gross weight was 23,000 pounds. Although the YF-17 lost the LWF/ACF competition, it was later resuscitated as the larger and heavier carrier-based McDonnell Douglas/Northrop F/A-18A/B Hornet for the U.S. Navy. And in essence, the YF-17 still lives today in the still larger and heavier carrier-based Boeing F/A-18E/F Super Hornet, which recently entered into service. *NASA*

On 23 December 1974, Rockwell test pilot Charles Bock piloted the first of four B-1As on its maiden flight, from Palmdale to Edwards. It was powered by four afterburning 30,000-pound-thrust class General Electric F101-GE-100 turbofan-jet engines, which gave it a top speed of Mach 2.2. It is 150 feet 2.5 inches long, 33 feet 7.25 inches high with a fully extended wingspan of 136 feet 8.5 inches (78 feet 2.5 inches swept back); gross weight was 389,800 pounds. Rockwell had built the four B-1A aircraft in hope that the aircraft would supplement and replace some models of the venerable B-52, but in 1977 President Carter canceled the B-1A program. The B-1 program was later resuscitated by President Reagan in the form of the B-1B Lancer. *Rockwell*

McDonnell Douglas built two YC-15 airplanes for the U.S. Air Force advanced medium short takeoff and landing transport) (AMST) program. The first one made its maiden 2-hour and 26-minute flight on 26 August 1975 from Long Beach to Edwards, piloted by U.S. Air Force test pilot Major John Harris. The YC-15 was powered by four nonaugmented 16,000-pound-thrust Pratt & Whitney JT8D-17 turbofan jet engines. It is 124 feet 3 inches long, 43 feet 4 inches high and has a wingspan of 110 feet 4 inches; gross takeoff weight was 219,180 pounds. The second YC-15 made its first flight on 5 December 1975. Although the YC-15 performed well, neither it nor its competitor, the Boeing YC-14, was ever ordered into production. Today's Boeing (formerly McDonnell Douglas) C 17A Globemaster III is a direct outgrowth of the YC-15. *AFFTC/HO*

Boeing also built two demonstrators for the U.S. Air Force AMST program. Designated YC-14, the first example made its 1-hour and 35-minute first flight at Seattle, Washington, on 9 August 1976 and later transferred to Edwards AFB on 11 November 1976. The second YC-14 first flew on 21 October 1976 and arrived at Edwards two days earlier on 9 November 1976. Both YC-14 airplanes were powered by two nonafterburning 50,000–pound-thrust-class General Electric F103-GE-100 turbofan jet engines. They measured 131 feet 8 inches in length, 48 feet 4 inches in height and have wingspans of 129 feet; gross takeoff weight was 117,500 pounds. The YC-14 versus the YC 15 AMST fly-off competition ended on 8 August 1977. Altogether, the two YC 14s and two YC 15s accumulated about 1,400 flying hours in some 700 flights. *AFFTC/HO*

Although the Northrop YF-17 lost out to the General Dynamics YF-16 in the 1974 LWF competition, many thought it deserved better. So taking the basic YF-17 matrix, McDonnell Douglas molded it into a larger and heavier design optimized for aircraft carrier duties. The U.S. Navy liked what it saw and ordered the new design—now designated F/A-18 and named Hornet—into limited production. McDonnell Douglas test pilot Jack Krings completed the first flight of the premier McDonnell Douglas F/A-18A Hornet on 18 November 1978 at Lambert Field in St. Louis, Missouri. A number of other single- and tandem-seat full-scale development (FSD) Hornets followed, and after their respective flight test and armament evaluations, the type went into full-scale production. The single-seat F/A-18A is powered by two augmented 16,000–pound-thrust-class General Electric F404-GE-400 turbofan engines, which gives it its Mach 1.8 top speed. The original single-seat Hornet is 56 feet long, 15 feet 3.5 inches high with a wingspan of 40 feet 5in; gross takeoff weight is 49,225 pounds. *U.S. Navy*

Northrop test pilot Russell Scott is shown here making a successful first flight of the No. 1 Northrop F-20 Tigershark on 30 August 1982 at Edwards AFB, effortlessly hitting Mach 1.04. Two more F-20s were completed, and they made their first flights at Edwards respectively on 26 August 1983 and 6 May 1984. The F-20 was to have been the Mach 2 follow-on to the Mach 1 Northrop F-5E/F Tigershark series. It was privately funded by Northrop itself in an attempt to sell lightweight fighters to American allies and friends. However, these allies and friends preferred the F-16 Fighting Falcon, and no F-20 production orders were forthcoming. The F-20 was powered by a single augmented 18,000-pound–thrust-class F404-GE-100 turbofan jet engine. The Tigershark was 47 feet 4 inches long, 13 feet 10 inches high and has a wingspan of 26 feet 8 inches; gross weight was 28,000 pounds. It's been called one of the best fighters built that never went into production. *AFFTC/HO*

The premier tilt-rotor Bell/Boeing V-22 Osprey vertical/short takeoff and landing (V/STOL) made a successful first flight at Dallas, Texas, on 19 March 1989. It takes off and lands like a helicopter and flies like an airplane at speeds of up to 315 miles per hour—about 120 miles per hour more than a helicopter. It is powered by two 6,150-shaft-horsepower Allison T406-AD-400 gas turbine engines that spin very large 38-foot-diameter three-bladed propellers. It is 57 feet 3.96 inches long, 17 feet 11 inches high, and has a wingspan of 83 feet 9.60 inches; gross weight is 47,500 pounds (vertical takeoff). It meets the needs of all U.S. armed forces and is scheduled for full-scale production in the year 2005. *Bell Helicopter Textron*

Scaled Composites built three unoccupied X-38 crew return vehicles (CRV) for NASA. The first example, known as V131, made its first flight at Edwards AFB on 12 March 1998. The subscale X-38 is 24.5 feet long and 8.4 feet high, and has a maximum width of 11.6 feet. It is approximately 80 percent the size of the once-planned operational crew return vehicle. During atmospheric tests at NASA's Dryden facility at Edwards, V131 was dropped from a pylon under the wing of a B-52 at altitudes varying from 25,000 to 45,000 feet, after which a parachute deployed to safely return it to Rogers Dry Lake. Although the X-38 program was canceled, an operational CRV based on the X-38 would have been used to ferry astronauts back to earth from the International Space Station. *NASA*

The one-of-a-kind unoccupied Boeing X-40A space maneuver vehicle (SMV) performed a series of autonomous, precision approach and landing tests at Holloman AFB, New Mexico, beginning on 11 August 1998. The X-40A, similar in shape and size to the X-37, made seven successful autonomous landings after being dropped from a CH-47 helicopter from varying altitudes. The X-40A is a fully instrumented X-vehicle that supports the flight dynamics of the proposed and similarly shaped Mach 25 Boeing X-37 reusable spaceplane, which was to serve as a test bed for 41 different airframe structure, propulsion system, and operations technologies designed to lower the cost of access to space. The X-40A is an 80 percent-scale version of the 27.5-foot-long X-37. *NASA*

The Boeing EA-18 airborne electronic attack (AEA) variant of the two-seat F/A-18F Super Hornet made its first flight on 16 November 2001 at St. Louis, Missouri. Now designated the EA 18G AEA variant and unofficially named Growler, if it goes into production, it is to begin replacing the U.S. Navy fleet of EA-6B Prowler aircraft in 2009. The EA 18G has the same propulsion system and measurements as the F/A 18F but carries a sophisticated suite of electronic and weapons to jam and kill enemy radar stations and surface-to-air missile sites. *U.S. Air Force*

chapter five

MANNED VS. UNMANNED FLIGHT

SUDDENLY, AFTER THE SUCCESSFUL first flight of the Northrop B-2 Advanced Technology Bomber in July 1989, America had a stealth bomber and a stealth fighter. But as advanced as these two aircraft were, a number of other interesting aircraft development programs, using both manned and unmanned aircraft, were afoot. In the early- to mid-1990s these sophisticated new aircraft began to make their appearances, first in the shape of the manned YF-22A and YF-23A advanced tactical fighter (ATF) prototypes. These were followed in July 1994 by the unmanned RQ-1A Predator, the first modern unmanned aerial vehicle (UAV). The RQ-1A and a number of subsequent UAVs were in development to serve primarily as reconnaissance aircraft in real time and near–real time combat. In addition, the RQ-1A, armed with two AGM-114 Hellfire air-to-ground guided missiles, served as an unmanned combat aerial vehicle (UCAV). Now, with the advent of the X-45A "Shrike" and X-47A Pegasus, both being developed under dedicated UCAV programs, UAVs are being built as out-and-out combat aircraft.

Manned Aircraft
On 27 August 1990, Northrop test pilot Paul Metz made a successful flight of the first of two YF-23As at Edwards Air Force Base. Just more than a month later, Lockheed test pilot David Ferguson made a successful flight of the first of two YF-22As from Palmdale to Edwards Air Force Base.

Unmanned Aerial Vehicles
From the mid-1990s to today, the newest rage in aircraft development has been creating unmanned, or unoccupied, aerial vehicles. These are designed mainly for long endurance, real time war aerial reconnaissance. But some of these, namely the

General Atomics RQ-1 Predator, have been configured to carry and fire air-to-ground missiles, such as the antitank Hellfire missile. The first RQ-1A Predator made a successful first flight on 3 July 1994 at an undisclosed location. Since then, on numerous occasions, Predators have been used in combat—most recently in Operation Iraqi Freedom.

Since the advent of the Predator, a number of other UAVs have been brought on line. These include the Pioneer UAV Inc. RQ-2 Pioneer, the Northrop Grumman RQ-4 Global Hawk, and Israel Aircraft Industries' Malat RQ-5 Hunter. All of these UAVs have served in combat.

Even though the Predator has served as an armed UAV, it is not a dedicated unmanned or unoccupied combat aerial vehicle (UCAV). Two UCAVs are currently in development.

Unmanned Combat Aerial Vehicles

Both the U.S. Air Force and U.S. Navy are hard at work to establish operational fleets of unmanned combat aerial vehicles (UCAV) in the not-so-distant future. In fact, two experimental UCAV hopefuls, the Boeing X-45A "Shrike" and the Northrop Grumman X-47A Pegasus, already have taken wing at their respective flight test locations.

As currently projected, an operational UCAV would incorporate side-by-side weapons bays to house the latest in precision-guided weapons, such as the satellite-guided joint direct attack munitions that proved so successful in Operation Iraqi Freedom. Moreover, these stealthy unoccupied UCAVs would be used in first-strike scenarios in which specific high-threat targets, such as radar stations and surface-to-air missile sites, had to be destroyed. They also would be used in other critical operations, such as the suppression of enemy communication and command-and-control functions.

One day, as the UCAV concept matures, the planes might even be used for air-to-air combat, removing fighter pilots from the danger zone. And larger versions could even be used as long-range strategic bombers. All this remains to be seen, however, but so far these experimental UCAVs are beginning to turn some important heads.

Under the highly classified Senior Trend program, five full-scale development (FSD) YF-117A airplanes were built and flown to take up where the XST aircraft had left off. The first YF-117A, piloted by Lockheed test pilot Harold Farley, made a successful first flight on 18 June 1981 at Groom Dry Lake. These five service-test examples led to the production of 59 operational F-117As. A 60th F-117A—actually the first production example—was built, but prior to U.S. Air Force acceptance, it crashed to destruction upon its first takeoff on 20 April 1982 and was never counted in the stealth fighter production inventory. The F-117A Nighthawk is powered by two nonafterburning 10,800–pound-thrust General Electric F404 GE-F1D2 turbofan jet engines. It is 65 feet 11 inches long, 12 feet 5 inches high, and has a wingspan of 43 feet 4 inches; gross weight is 52,500 pounds. The F-117A Nighthawk holds the unique distinction of being the world's first low observable or stealth combat airplane, and its prowess was realized during Operation Desert Storm in 1991. *Lockheed Martin Skunk Work*s

The Lockheed experimental survivable testbed (XST) can lay claim to being the world's first low-observable-technology, or stealth, airplane. It was developed under the highly classified U.S. Air Force Have Blue program, and two examples were built and flown at Groom Dry Lake on the Nellis Air Force Base complex in Nevada, sometimes referred to as the "Ranch" or "Area 51." The first example, with Lockheed test pilot William Park at the controls, made its first flight on 1 December 1977; it flew another 35 times, crashing on its 36th flight. U.S. Air Force Major Norman Dyson was the first to fly the second example, on 20 July 1978; it flew another 51 times, crashing on its 52nd flight. These were nonlethal crashes, but both XST examples were lost. Nevertheless, they were successful enough during their respective flight test programs to prove the worth of stealth aircraft, which in turn led to the creation of the Lockheed Martin F-117A Nighthawk—the world's first operational stealth airplane. *Lockheed Martin Skunk Work*s

Two highly maneuverable aircraft technology (HiMAT) subscale air vehicles were built as remotely piloted research vehicles (RPRV) to demonstrate the maneuverability of a 1990s conceptual fighter-type aircraft. The first example made its first flight on 27 August 1979 at Edwards AFB after being air-launched by a B-52 mother ship at 45,000 feet. Each one of the joint NASA/U.S. Air Force HiMAT air vehicles was powered by a single augmented 5,000-pound-thrust-class General Electric J85-GE-21 turbojet engine, which gave them a top speed of 925 miles per hour at 45,000 feet during their respective flight test programs. The HiMAT air vehicle is 23 feet long with a wingspan of 16 feet. These 3,400-pound RPRVs experienced a maximum load factor of 8g during numerous of their respective transonic speed-regime (600–800 miles per hour) flight tests in the early 1980s. *NASA*

The premier Northrop (now Northrop Grumman) B-2A advanced technology bomber (ATB), now officially named Spirit, made its first flight on 17 July 1989 from Palmdale to Edwards AFB. Northrop test pilot Bruce Hinds was in the left seat, and U.S. Air Force test pilot Colonel Richard Couch was in the right seat. The B-2A is 69 feet long and 17 feet high, with a wingspan of 172 feet; gross weight is 336,500 pounds. It has four nonaugmented 17,300-pound-thrust General Electric F118-GE-100 turbofan-jet engines that give it a high subsonic top speed of about Mach 0.8. Northrop Grumman built a total of 21 B-2A Spirit stealth bombers, and they are operated by the 509th Bomb Wing of the Air Combat Command. Coincidentally, the B-2A has the identical 172-foot wingspan of the Northrop YB-49 Flying Wing bomber, which made its debut in 1947. *Northrop Grumman*

Lockheed Martin and Boeing built two stealthy tactical reconnaissance RQ-3A Dark Star unmanned aerial vehicles as Tier III minus high altitude endurance (HAE) demonstrators. The first example made a successful first flight at Edwards AFB on 29 March 1996. With a wingspan of 69 feet, an operational RQ-3A was to fly above 45,000 feet at subsonic speeds on missions lasting more than eight hours. The first example crashed on its second flight in April 1996, and after an investigation and modifications, the second example made a successful first flight on 29 June 1998. The RQ-3A is 15 feet long and 3 feet 6 inches high; gross weight is 8,500 pounds. It is powered by a single nonaugmented 1,900-pound-thrust Williams research/Rolls-Royce FJ44-1A turbofan engine, which gives it a cruising speed of about 290 miles per hour. Two additional Dark Stars were built but never flown, and the RQ-3A program was canceled in December 1999. *Lockheed Martin*

In the fall of 1996, Boeing test pilot Rudy Haug made the first flight on the *Bird of Prey* technology demonstrator, so named because of its gull-like wings. Through the year 1999 another 37 test flights were successfully flown by Haug and several other test pilots. This program, funded entirely by Boeing itself ($67 million), was so secret it was not made public until 18 October 2002, some three years after flight testing had ended. It used a single 3,000-pound-thrust-class Pratt & Whitney JT15D-5C turbofan engine for its propulsion system, which allowed it to reach its maximum operating speed of 300 miles per hour and maximum altitude of 20,000 feet. The stealthy air vehicle is 47 feet long, has a span of about 23 feet and weighs just about 7,400 pounds. Among other things, the unique *Bird of Prey* pioneered the use of large, single-piece aircraft structures. *Boeing Phantom Works*

The 28 percent-scale Boeing Phantom Works X-36 tailless agility research aircraft, a pilotless demonstrator, made its first flight on 17 May 1997 at Edwards AFB. The X-36 is 18 feet long, 3 feet high, and 10 feet wide at its widest point; gross weight is 1,250 pounds. It is powered by a single nonafterburning 700-pound-thrust Williams Research F112 turbofan engine. In a six-month period, the X-36 made 25 successful flight tests. With neither vertical nor horizontal tail planes, it performed very well indeed. Two identical X-36 air vehicles were built. In operational action as an advanced fighter, a tailless fighter based on the configuration of the X-36 would feature less weight, drag, and radar cross-section. *NASA*

The 7 September 1997 first flight of EMD F-22A Raptor No. 1 with Paul Metz at the controls transformed the Advanced Tactical Fighter program—launched by the USAF in October 1986—into the Air Dominance Fighter program of the new century. Powered by two 35,000-pound thrust class Pratt & Whitney F119-PW-100 turbofan engines the 2.5-plus Mach Raptor can *supercruise* to speeds in excess of 1.5 Mach without the use of afterburners. Moreover, with its first-look/first-shoot/first-kill capability, operational Raptors can decide the outcome of aerial battles even before their opponents are aware they are there. In its desire to replace its aging fleet of F-15 Eagle air superiority fighters, the USAF plans to procure 339 Raptors through the year 2010. Recently redesignated as F/A-22 to better describe its versatility as a multirole fighter, the Lockheed Martin/Boeing Raptor is even stealthier than Lockheed Martin's own F-117A Nighthawk. The F/A-22s are being built at Lockheed Martin's Marietta, Georgia facility. *Lockheed Martin*

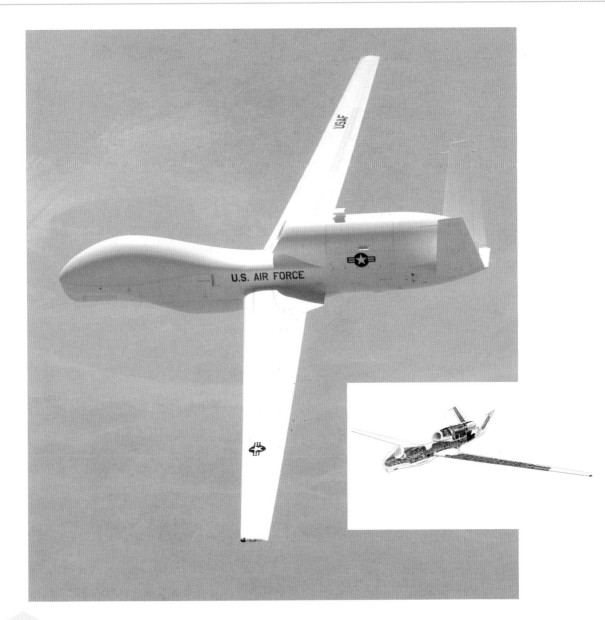

The unmanned aerial vehicle (UAV), now known as the Northrop Grumman (formerly Teledyne Ryan) RQ-4A Global Hawk, made a successful first flight at Edwards AFB on 28 February 1998. Constructed of composite materials, the RQ-4A Global Hawk is 44 feet long and 15 feet high, with a wingspan of more than 116 feet; gross takeoff weight is 25,600 pounds. Once mission parameters are programmed into Global Hawk, this operational and combat-proven UAV can autonomously taxi, take off, fly, remain on station to capture near-real-time and real-time imagery, return, and land. Ground-based operators monitor its health and status throughout its mission, with the ability to change navigation and reconnaissance-sensor plans during flight as required. Global Hawk's unrefueled range is 13,500 miles, its endurance is more than 35 hours, and its operating altitude can exceed 65,000 feet with a 2,000-pound payload. It is powered by a single 7,100-pound-thrust Allison (now Rolls-Royce) AE 3007H turbofan engine, and its top speed is 450 miles per hour. *Northrop Grumman*

The first Northrop Grumman RQ-8 Fire Scout made a successful first flight on 19 May 2001 at the Naval Air Systems command facility at its Western Test Range Complex in California. This vertical takeoff and landing UAV (or VTUAV) is 16.6 feet long and 9.7 feet high. It is powered by a single Rolls-Royce 250-C20W gas turbine engine. Its basic airframe was manufactured by Schweizer Aircraft Corporation, and Northrop Grumman added its unique autonomous-flight systems and finalized its manufacture. The Fire Scout is a dedicated helicopter made of carbon-fiber composite materials and aluminum. *Northrop Grumman*

The first of two Boeing X-45A UCAV technology demonstrators made a successful first flight on 22 May 2002 from the NASA-DFRF at Edwards AFB. The second example made its first flight on 21 November 2002. These two air vehicles are powered by single 6,300-pound-thrust Honeywell F124 turbofan engines; they are tailless, and measure 26.5 feet in length with a wingspan of 33.8 feet. These unmanned combat aerial vehicle demonstrators were built and flown to investigate the technologies required to field operational and fully autonomous UCAVs to be used in future high-threat combat environments. A larger follow-on X-45B UCAV, scheduled to fly sometime in 2005, is to be the precursor of operational UCAVs after 2010. The X-45B is to be powered by a single General Electric F404-102D turbofan engine and carry two 2,000-pound precision-guided bombs in two side-by-side weapons bays. *NASA*

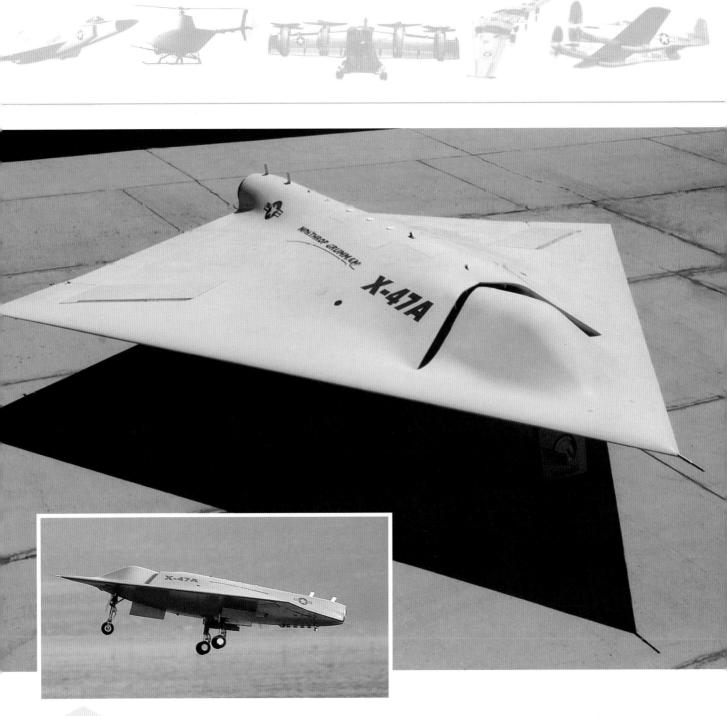

Having completed its low-, medium- and high-speed taxi tests by late 2002, the first of two Northrop Grumman X-47A Pegasus UCAV air vehicles made a successful first flight at the Naval Air Warfare Center—Weapons Division, China Lake, California, on 23 February 2003. The kite-shaped X-47A, powered by a single 3,200-pound-thrust Pratt & Whitney JT15D turbofan engine, is 27.9 feet long, with a nearly equal 27.8-foot wingspan. Pegasus was designed and built to demonstrate aerodynamic flying qualities suitable for aircraft carrier operations. Specific objectives of the program included: (1) achieving good low-speed aerodynamic handling qualities; (2) demonstrating compatibility with carrier landing systems; (3) simulating landing arrestment; and (4) demonstrating an air vehicle management and architecture applicable to future UAVs. One of the first goals of the Pegasus flight test program was to demonstrate the aerodynamic qualities of an autonomous UAV that would actually allow it to operate from a carrier, reducing the risk of carrier operations of a future naval UCAV system. This was critical to the future creation of a larger X-47B demonstrator, the forerunner of a combat-capable carrier-based UCAV. *Northrop Grumman*

The No. 1 Northrop YF-23A Gray Ghost (one of two unofficial names; the other being Black Widow II) made its first flight at Edwards AFB on 27 August 1990 with Northrop test pilot Paul Metz in charge. The second was first piloted by Northrop test pilot Jim Sandberg at Edwards on 26 October 1990. The No. 1 YF-23A was powered by two augmented 30,000-pound-thrust class Pratt & Whitney YF119-PW-100 turbofan engines, while No. 2 featured a pair of 30,000-pound-thrust class General Electric YF120-GE-100 augmented turbofan engines. Featuring supercruise, through which supersonic speeds can be achieved without augmentation, the GE-powered YF-23A achieved a still-classified speed of Mach 1.8-plus during one of its flight tests. *AFFTC/HO*

Two X-31 enhanced fighter maneuverability (EFM) airplanes were built by Rockwell International/North American Aircraft and Deutsche Aerospace (formerly MBB or Messerschmitt-Bolkow-Blohm) at Rockwell's Palmdale, California, facility. The first example, with Rockwell test pilot Ken Dyson under the canopy, made its first flight on 11 October 1990, from Palmdale to Edwards. The second example, also flying from Palmdale to Edwards, first flew on 19 January 1991. These two aircraft were powered by single nonaugmented 16,000-pound-thrust class General Electric F404-GE-400 turbofan jet engines. Both aircraft are 43 feet 3 inches long, 14 feet 5 inches high with wingspans of 23 feet 8 inches; gross weight is 16,100 pounds. Together, during the EFM flight test program, the X-31s completed 108 test flights. On 29 April 1993 the No. 2 X-31 successfully executed a minimum radius, 180-degree turn using a poststall maneuver, flying well beyond the aerodynamic limits of a conventional aircraft. The revolutionary maneuver has been dubbed the "Herbst maneuver," after Wolfgang Herbst, a German proponent of using poststall flight in air-to-air combat. *NASA*

Two Lockheed/Boeing/General Dynamics YF-22A Lightning IIs (unofficial name) were built to compete against the YF-23As in the advanced tactical fighter (ATF) competition. The first example of the YF-22A to fly, ship No. 2, was powered by two augmented 30,000–pound-thrust-class General Electric YF120-GE-100 turbofan engines. It made its first flight (Palmdale to Edwards AFB) on 29 August 1990 with Lockheed test pilot David Ferguson in the seat. The No. 1 YF-22A was first flown by Lockheed test pilot Tom Morgenfeld on 30 October 1990, from Palmdale to Edwards. The aircraft was powered by two augmented 30,000–pound-thrust-class Pratt & Whitney YF119-PW-100 turbofan engines. It had been scheduled to fly first, but late delivery of its two YF119 engines caused the delay. The ATF fly-off competition resulted in the YF119-powered YF-22A being declared the winner. That announcement was made on 23 April 1991. *AFFTC/HO*

The Boeing X32A Joint Strike Fighter (JSF) Conventional Takeoff and Landing (CTOL) Concept Demonstrator made a successful maiden flight on 18 September 2001. It was piloted by Boeing test pilot Fred Knox, who flew from Boeing's Phantom Works facility at Palmdale to Edwards AFB. The X-32A was powered by a single augmented 40,000-pound thrust class Pratt & Whitney F119-C turbofan engine. The X-32A is a 46 feet long, 13 feet 4 inches high with a wingspan of 36 feet. *Boeing*

The Lockheed Martin X-35A JSF CTOL Concept Demonstrator made a successful first flight from Palmdale to Edwards AFB on 24 October 2000, with Lockheed Martin test pilot Tom Morgenfield in the cockpit. The X-35A was powered by a single augmented 40,000-pound thrust class Pratt & Whitney F119-611C turbofan engine. The X-35A is 50 feet 11 inches long, 13 feet high with a wingspan of 33 feet. *Lockheed Martin*

On 15 November 2000 the Boeing X-32A began a series of flight tests to demonstrate JSF U.S. Navy carrier version (CV) handling qualities, especially field carrier landing practice (FCLP) maneuvers. Piloted by USN Commander Phillip "Rowdy" Yates, the X-32A was powered by a single augmented 40,000-pound thrust class Pratt & Whitney F119-611C turbo engine, which easily shot it to near 2 Mach speed during flight-test operations. *Boeing*

The Lockheed Martin X-35B JSF STOVL Concept Demonstrator made its first flight on 23 June 2001 with Lockheed Martin test pilot Simon Hargreaves at the helm. On 9 July 2001 it made a vertical takeoff from Palmdale, transitioned to flight mode, completed a supersonic flight, and landed at Edwards Air Force Base. The X-35B was 50 feet 11 inches long, 13 feet high with a wingspan of 33ft. It was powered by a single augmented 40,000-lb thrust Pratt & Whitney F119-611S turbofan engine. This lift fan, fitted vertically in the midsection of the fuselage, was engine-driven. Working in concert with the swiveling exhaust pipe, the lift fan provided more than adequate thrust to help launch and land, and will be used for the future operational F-35B STOVL aircraft for the USMC and Great Britain. *Lockheed Martin*

Lockheed Martin test pilot Joe Sweeny flew the X-35C JSF CV airplane to Edwards from Palmdale on 16 December 2001 to complete its first flight. The X-35C has the same dimensions as the X-34A/35B but with a wingspan of 40 feet. The production version of the X-35C, the F-35C, will ultimately replace a number of USN carrier-borne warplanes including the F/A-18C Hornet, currently active as a multi-role fighter/attack aircraft. On 26 October 2001 the Department of Defense selected the team of Lockheed Martin, Northrop Grumman, and BAE SYSTEMS as the winner of the JSF program. On that date, the designations F-35A, F-35B, and F-35C were issued, and the three JSF propulsive systems became the Pratt & Whitney F135-PW-200, -400 and -600. *Lockheed Martin*

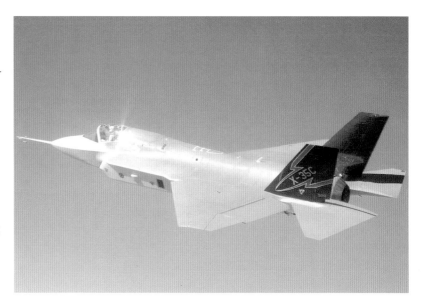

Under an international flight-test program, the Boeing Phantom Works X-31A Vectoring ESTOL (extremely short takeoff and landing) Control and Tailless Operational Research (VECTOR) aircraft Phase II program began at NAS PAX River, Maryland, with a successful first flight occurring on 17 May 2002. The earlier X-31A VECTOR Phase I operations held between February and April 2001 was implemented to make sure the X-31, having been in storage for five years after its EFM program had ended, was properly restored and flight-test ready. The Phase II X-31A VECTOR program demonstrated simulated ESTOL operations in the air. The Phase III operations—actual ESTOL runway demonstrations—began in the fall of 2002. The X-31A VECTOR has the same configuration as the X-31 EFM but with different internal systems and computer software. *Boeing Phantom Works*

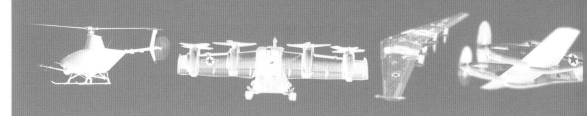

chapter six

FUTURE X-PLANES

THE FIRST CENTURY of manned flight has generated a cornucopia of piston-, turbojet- and rocket-powered air vehicles. As far as all-out performance goes, this development has culminated with the fleet of NASA space shuttles.

While the space shuttles are not X-Planes, they certainly could never have been built and flown without the vast libraries of knowledge that have been generated by the large variety of X-Planes during the past 100 years. In fact, as recently as the year 1961, when President John F. Kennedy announced that the United States would land men on the Moon and safely return them to Earth before the year 1970, nobody believed such a feat would be possible in their lifetime.

Ongoing and Future Endeavors

So what does the next century of flight hold for mankind? Will it include manned trips to Mars? Only time will tell. But if the future of flight progresses as rapidly as the past adventures in flight have, just about anything will become feasible. But all of this continues to depend on the developmental and experimental aircraft and spacecraft discussed below.

The Lockheed Martin/Boeing team continues to produce Pratt & Whitney F119-powered F/A-22 Raptor air dominance fighter aircraft for the U.S. Air Force. At this writing, nine engineering, manufacturing, and development (EMD) Raptors have been built and flown. Additionally, two production representative test vehicle (PRTV) F/A-22s have flown, while six low-rate initial production (LRIP) Raptors are in various stages of manufacturing. Whether the F/A-22 Raptor goes into full-scale production depends on the success of these 17 EMD, PRTV, and LRIP aircraft. And so far, according to all reports, their performance is exemplary.

The proposed full-scale and piloted NASA X-44A multiaxis no-tail aircraft (MANTA) would be based on the Lockheed Martin F/A-22 Raptor's airframe, propulsion system, and avionics. The X-44A would have a large delta wing and dedicated multiaxis, thrust-vectoring exhaust nozzles, but not horizontal or vertical tails. Whether it is built and flown remains to be seen. *Lockheed Martin*

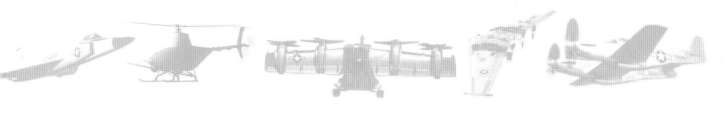

The Lockheed Martin F-35 series of CTOL (conventional takeoff and landing), CV (carrier version), and STOVL (short takeoff and vertical landing) joint strike fighter (JSF) aircraft now are in the systems development and demonstration phase at the Fort Worth, Texas, division of Lockheed Martin. In the systems development and demonstration phase, Lockheed Martin in Fort Worth will build 14 F-35s: 5 F-35A CTOLs, 5 F-35C CVs, and 4 F-35B STOVL airframes for flight test evaluations. The first example, a U.S. Air Force CTOL F-35A, is scheduled to make its initial flight on 28 August 2005. In early 2006 the U.S. Marine Corps/RAF/RN STOVL F-35B is scheduled to fly, while in late 2006 the U.S. Navy CV F-35C is to take wing. For other important tests, such as radar signature and structural and fatigue demonstrations, another eight ground-based F-35s will be built.

As of this writing, the F-35B is expected to reach its initial operational capability (IOC) with the U.S. Marine Corps in 2010; the F-35A of the U.S. Air Force in 2011; and the F-35C of the U.S. Navy in 2012. Current with this publication, the U.S. Air Force is expected to buy 1,763 F-35As; the U.S. Marine Corps, 609 F-35Bs; the Royal Air Force, 90 F-35Bs; the Royal Navy, 60 F-35Bs; and the U.S. Navy, 480 F-35Cs.

A number of other nations—Australia, Canada, Denmark, Israel, Netherlands, Norway, and Turkey—may purchase still another 500 to 600 join strike fighters, for a total of 3,502 to 3,602. Moreover, two different propulsion systems will be validated. These are the Pratt & Whitney F135 and the General Electric F136 turbofan engines, rated in the 40,000-pound-thrust class.

Projected Air Vehicles

With the ongoing developments in advanced aerodynamics and propulsive systems, computerized fly-by-light and fly-by-wire flight-control systems, and a host of other ongoing and upcoming technological advances in the field of aerospace, the forthcoming generations of manned and unmanned air vehicles will be more than just a little interesting. Some of these projected air vehicles are from the following companies and agencies:

• Northrop Grumman

In late 2002, the integrated systems sector of Northrop Grumman Corporation unveiled a design for an efficient and capable long range supersonic cruise aircraft that would operate with a less intense supersonic boom.

The design, which includes variants for a long-range military-strike aircraft and a civil-business jet, is part of Northrop Grumman's work under the Defense Advanced Research Projects Agency's (DARPA) Quiet Supersonic Platform (QSP) program.

The concept calls for a joined-wing air vehicle that is 156 feet long with a 58-foot wingspan. It features a dorsal (top-mounted), active, isentropic engine air-inlet system, extensive laminar-flow aerodynamics, and wings with an adaptive (shape-shifting, if you will) leading edge. The preferred concept meets DARPA's goals of 0.3 pound per square foot initial sonic boom overpressure (approximately seven times lower than that of the Concorde SST), a speed greater than Mach 2 (about 1,480 miles per hour) and a range of 6,900 miles.

• Lockheed Martin

In March 2002 DARPA also awarded Lockheed Martin a Phase II contract to continue work on its version of the quiet supersonic platform.

• Lawrence Livermore National Laboratory

(LLNL) is working with DARPA to eventually build and fly a reusable hypersonic (Mach 10, 6,700 miles per hour) system known as the HyperSoar air vehicle. The current design for the HyperSoar features a 213-foot-long airframe with a maximum width of 79 feet. As a wave rider–type of air vehicle, HyperSoar craft would skip along the higher reaches of Earth's atmosphere during its flight profile. As envisaged, HyperSoar would take off horizontally from a runway of at least 10,000 feet in length, climb to 115,000 feet, engage its propulsion system, and then operate at between 115,000 and 200,000 feet. The aircraft would literally skip upward to its maximum altitude after it had lost too much altitude during its wave-riding flight profile. In other words, as its altitude decreases to its lowest limit—115,000 feet, or its skip altitude, about every 248.5 miles—it can skip back up to 200,000 feet; the skip is said to be only a 1.5-G maneuver.

If applicable, an operational HyperSoar air vehicle could be used as a strategic bomber, reconnaissance/strike platform, and even a transport in the future. The bomber version could carry nearly 100,000 pounds of ordnance with a combat radius of 6,200 miles.

• Boeing Phantom Works
This branch of Boeing is studying a blended wing body (BWB) aircraft concept that may be employed in the future as a multirole platform.

That is, it could be used for any number of missions, including a passenger-carrying jetliner, tanker-transport, and even as a weapons platform. The BWB aircraft concept offers greater structural, aerodynamic, and operating efficiencies than today's conventional tube-and-wing designs. In other words, a BWB aircraft would have greater range and improved fuel economy.

The Boeing Phantom Works has introduced a concept study known as the ultra large transport aircraft (ULTRA), which it calls the Pelican. The ULTRA would measure some 300 feet in length and have a 500-foot wingspan and a wing area exceeding an acre. It would be powered by four very high thrust turbopropjet engines spinning special high-pull eight-bladed propellers. It would be nearly twice as large as today's largest airplane, the Russian An-225, and could carry up to five times its payload—as much as 1.5 million pounds of cargo.

The proposed but as yet unnamed NASA morphing airplane will use a technology first patented by the
Wright brothers: wing warping. NASA will work on the morphing airplane concept with Lockheed
Martin, and the project is classified secret. Other than the fact that the unique air vehicle will be able
to change shape in flight, there is little else known about it at this particular writing. *NASA*

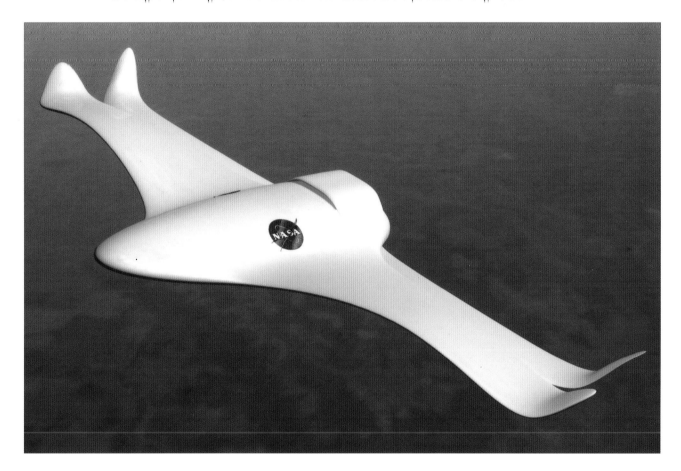

The proposed Boeing Pelican is a high-capacity cargo-carrying transport airplane concept being studied by Boeing Phantom Works. It would be the biggest airplane in the history of aviation, with a length of more than 300 feet and have a wingspan of 500 feet. Being specifically designed as a long-range, transoceanic transport, the Pelican would fly as low as 20 feet above the sea, taking advantage of an aerodynamic phenomenon called ground effect, which reduces parasite drag and increases fuel economy. With a projected payload of 1.5 million pounds, the Pelican could fly 11,500 miles over water and 7,500 over land. Over land it would fly at altitudes of 20,000 feet and higher. *Boeing Phantom Works*

The four-crewmember orbital space plane (OSP) is a concept being studied to someday replace NASA's fleet of space shuttles under what is known as the NASA space launch initiative (SLI). Four airframe contractors—Boeing, Northrop Grumman, Lockheed Martin, and Orbital Sciences—are vying for the production contract to build the demonstrator. As currently projected, the proposed OSP would be carried aloft either by rocket-boost or atop an air vehicle prior to its orbital insertion burn under its own power. *NASA*

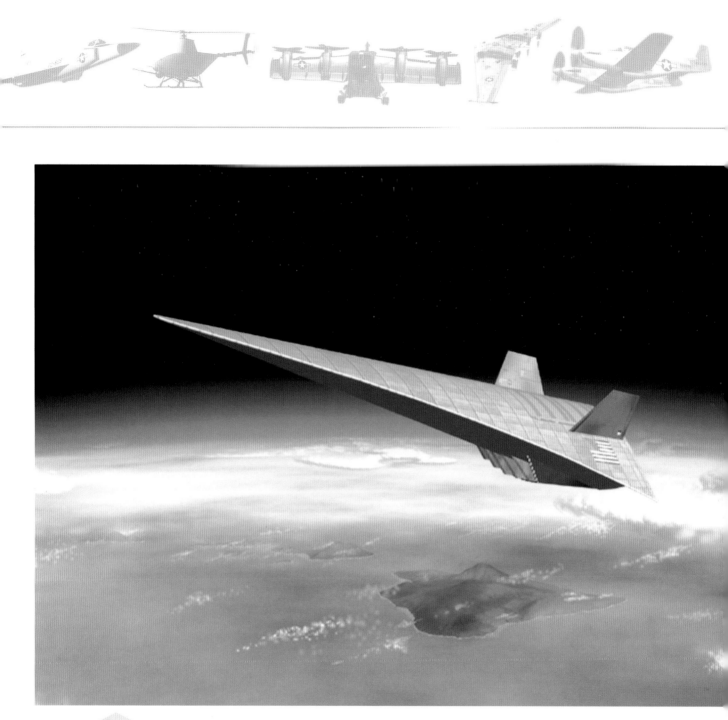

The proposed HyperSoar air vehicle is to be a hypersonic global range reconnaissance/strike system capable of a speed of 6,700 miles per hour (Mach 10). It could fly between any two points on the globe in less than two hours. As designed, the HyperSoar air vehicle would fly to an altitude of about 130,000 feet – outside the earth's atmosphere, and then skip along the edge of earth's atmosphere, much like a flat stone skips across water. As it reentered earth's atmosphere, it would fire its air-breathing engines to once more skip back into space. Approximately 25 such skips would be required on a flight from the Midwestern United States to Japan.
Lawrence Livermore National Laboratory

Two X-37 reusable spaceplane demonstrators are being built by Boeing Phantom Works for both atmospheric and orbital flight test evaluations. The first example, designed for atmospheric flight test, is known as the X-37 approach and landing test vehicle, and it was scheduled to fly in April 2004. The second example, known as the X-37 long-duration orbital vehicle, is scheduled to be placed in low Earth orbit by a Boeing Delta II rocket in July 2006. The X-37 is 27.5 feet long, with a wingspan of 15 feet. The first version of the X-37 will be air-launched at 45,000 feet by a NASA B-52H to perform an autonomous approach and landing at Edwards AFB. With the space shuttle *Columbia* tragedy in 2003, a new type of space transportation system based on the X-37 becomes more and more viable. *Boeing Phantom Works*

Boeing Phantom Works has built the X-50A Dragonfly air vehicle to exhibit high-speed, vertical takeoff and landing (VTOL) flight characteristics for the purpose of assessing and validating an advanced rotorcraft concept known as the canard/rotor wing (C/RW) technology. If the concept is proved in flight test evaluations, operational C/RW air vehicles would take off and land within confined areas, rapidly transition to and from a fixed-wing mode, and operate at speeds in excess of 460 miles per hour. Potential manned and unmanned missions for this type of air vehicle include armed escort, communications/data relay, logistics resupply, tactical air support, and reconnaissance. Two X-50A C/RW air vehicles have been built as unmanned subscale demonstrators. They measure 17.7 feet in length, 6.5 feet in height, and the rotor blades are 12 feet in diameter. They are powered by single 730-pound-thrust Williams International F112-WR-100 turbofan engine. At this writing, the first X-50A was scheduled to make its first flight sometime in 2003. *Boeing Phantom Works*

The NASA F/A-18A Hornet, modified to flight test the Boeing Phantom Works-developed active aeroelastic wing (AAW), made its first flight at Edwards AFB on 15 November 2002. This flexible wing borrows on the 1903 Wright Flyer technology known as wing warping, whereby flight control is accomplished through twisting or warping the wing to achieve roll control. NASA test pilot Dana Purifoy made the 68-minute test hop. During later test flights, aileron control was simulated by warping the AAW. NASA has several F/A-18 Hornet aircraft which it uses on a regular basis for a number of advanced aerodynamic conceptual flight test programs. The AAW employed on this F/A-18 is reminiscent of the F-111 MAW program in the mid-1980s. *NASA*

The Boeing YAL-1A airborne laser (ABL) made its first flight at Wichita, Kansas on 18 July 2002. It is based upon the 747-400F freighter version of the 747 jetliner and is powered by four General Electric CF6-80 turbofan-jet engines. It features a single Northrop Grumman high-energy laser (HEL) firing through a nose turret to destroy ballistic missiles while they are still in their boost phase. The high-energy laser itself is known as a megawatt chemical oxygen Iodine laser (COIL). The COIL on an operational AL-1A, based on the prototype attack laser, Model 1A (YAL-1A), is to have a maximum firing range of more than 200 miles. *U.S. Air Force*

In March 1999 the Defense Advanced Research Projects Agency (DARPA) awarded both Lockheed Martin and Northrop Grumman Phase II contracts to continue their respective studies on the proposed quiet supersonic platform (QSP) air vehicles. General Electric was also issued a Phase II funding for QSP propulsion system studies. The QSP air vehicles will be optimized to meet desired sonic boom goals while maximizing range and payload performance. The QSP program is focused on creating a viable long-range doublesonic aircraft with gross takeoff weight of 100,000 pounds, an unrefueled range of 6,000 miles, a cruise speed of Mach 2 to 2.4, with the capability of carrying a payload of at least 20,000 pounds. More important to the QSP air vehicle program is the requirement of an initial shock pressure rise of no more than 0.3 pounds per square foot to reduce its sonic boom signature – roughly one order of magnitude below what conventional supersonic aircraft (read: fighters) produce. *Northrop Grumman*

CONCLUSION

SO WHAT WILL the second century of manned flight bring about? Surely, for one thing, there will be an ever-increasing cadre of more and more sophisticated unmanned aircraft. But in the area of manned aircraft and spacecraft a number of thresholds still need to be crossed. One such barrier is the creation of a workable hypersonic civil transport capable of taking off like an airplane, reaching speeds of Mach 6–8 (4,450 to 5,900 miles per hour), then landing like an airplane—without shattering every window below it while it is en route. Another development on the horizon is designing an autonomous combat air vehicle that would no longer require pilots to be placed in mortal danger and provide safer commercial and private aircraft for the flying public.

Perhaps the foremost challenge to the aerospace industry in the twenty-first century is to create a spacecraft propulsion system that would allow for travel from Earth to any one of our own solar system's worlds in hours rather than years. Just imagine one day getting aboard an airliner-like spacecraft at a conventional airport, taking off, enjoying a grand tour of our own solar system during a 10-hour flight and then landing back on Earth at the same airport. Just imagine such a journey, during which the pilots of your spacecraft would take you to each and every one of the eight other planets in our solar system, circle it at least once to get a good view, and of course personal photographs, before returning to Earth. Science fiction you say? You bet it is, now. But before the 200th anniversary of manned flight comes about on 17 December 2103, such an excursion will most likely be fact rather than fantasy.

However, the foregoing cannot and will not happen unless America continues to design, develop, and exercise its current, upcoming, and future fleets of X-planes—both civilian and military—toward the visions of flight that will continue to grow ever closer to our vast horizons.

In the first century of human-controlled and self-propelled aircraft flight, mankind has successfully expanded the realms of aeronautics and astronautics to the high drama of landing 12 men on the Moon and safely returning them to Earth. And that was more than 30 years ago. In the years following those historic manned journeys through the space between the Earth and the Moon, the half-airplane, half-spaceship fleet of space shuttles was created. These space planes have successfully flown 111 missions to Earth orbit, and incredibly, working in concert, have greatly contributed to a multitude of scientific discoveries and to the ongoing construction of the International Space Station (ISS).

Out of 113 space shuttle missions, 111 have been successful. Two space shuttle missions—No. 25 [*Challenger*, 28 January 1986] and 113 [*Columbia*, 1 February 2003], were tragic failures. In each case, seven astronauts were lost. The former was lost during ascent, the latter during descent.

During the first 100 years of flight, then, while staying within Earth's own atmosphere, pilots have successfully flown airplanes from altitudes of a mere 20 feet to higher than 67 miles, distances from about 120 feet to around the world, and to speeds ranging from just 12 miles per hour to more than 4,500 miles per hour.

Mankind has celebrated a century of flight and continues to fly on toward the near and far horizons of aeronautical and astronautical explorations.

Appendix I
Some of the Most Significant Aerospace Milestones

— 17 December 1903, Wright Flyer, world's first human-controlled and self-propelled flight by a heavier-than-air vehicle
— 2 October 1942, Bell XP-59A Airacomet, America's first official flights of a manned turbojet-powered airplane
— 5 July 1944, Northrop N-12, America's first flight of a manned rocket-powered airplane
— 19 June 1947, Lockheed P-80R *Racey*, the highly modified, one-of-a-kind and redesignated XP-80B that set the world absolute speed record with a mark of 623.608 miles per hour, became the first U.S. plane to hold the speed record in 24 years

— 20 August 1947, Douglas D-558-1 Skystreak, U.S. Navy research airplane that established an official world absolute speed record of 640.743 miles per hour; increased that mark to 650.796 miles per hour on 25 August
— 14 October 1947, Bell X-1, Mach 1.06, world's first supersonic flight (faster than the speed of sound) established by a manned air vehicle
— 21 November 1947, North American XP-86 Sabre Jet, first supersonic flights by a nonresearch, turbojet-powered, combat-type airplane; in two separate flights, George Welch dove the XP-86 to Mach 1.02, then Mach 1.03 (There is ongoing undocumented belief than Welch had actually exceeded the speed of sound in a dive prior to 14 October 1947, but this remains to be proven).
— 20 November 1953, Douglas D-558-2 Skyrocket achieves Mach 2.005, world's first doublesonic

flight by a manned airplane
— 7 September 1956, Bell X-2 attains altitude of 125,907 feet, world's first flight above 100,000 feet by a manned airplane
— 27 September 1956, Bell X-2, Mach 3.196 (2,369.68 miles per hour), world's first triplesonic flight by a manned airplane
— 7 March 1961, North American X-15, Mach 4.43 (2,905 miles per hour), world's first quadrasonic flight by a manned airplane
— 12 September 1961, North American X-15 achieves Mach 5.27 (3,603 miles per hour), world's first hypersonic flight (Mach 5.0 and above) by a manned airplane
— 9 November 1961, North American X-15, Mach 6.04 (4,094 miles per hour), first flight by a manned airplane to exceed six times the speed of sound
— 30 April 1962, North American X-15 reaches altitude of 246,700 feet

(46.72 miles), world's first flight above 200,000 feet (37.87 miles) by a manned airplane

- 17 July 1962, North American X-15 attains altitude of 314,750 feet (59.6 miles), world's first flight above 300,000 feet (56.8 miles) by a manned airplane

- 22 August 1963, North American X-15 climbs to 354,200 feet (67.083 miles), world's highest flight by a manned airplane until the fleet of space shuttle orbital vehicles

- 19 March 1966, North American XB-70A Valkyrie reaches altitude of 74,000 feet (14 miles), highest altitude ever attained by a large and heavy bomber-type airplane

- 12 April 1966, North American XB-70A Valkyrie attains Mach 3.08 (2,283.68 miles per hour), highest speed ever attained by a large and heavy bomber type airplane

- 3 October 1967, North American X-15A-2 achieves Mach 6.70 (4,520 miles per hour), world's fastest flight by a manned airplane until the fleet of space shuttle orbital vehicles

- 24 December 1968, Apollo 8, first manned orbiting flight around the Moon by three NASA astronauts

- 20 July 1969, Apollo 11, first manned landing upon the Moon by two NASA astronauts; liftoff 16 July, splashdown 24 July

- 18 February 1970, Northrop HL-10, the highest-ever speed of any of the lifting-body type of air vehicles was attained at Mach 1.86

- 12 April to 14 April 1981, Space shuttle Columbia, first rocket-launched and runway-recovered mission of a manned Earth-orbiting vehicle; mission duration 2 days,

6 hours, 20 minutes, 53 seconds

- 13 September 1985, a modified McDonnell Douglas F-15A Eagle fired an antisatellite (ASAT) missile and destroyed a satellite orbiting 340 miles above the Earth

- 14 December to 23 December 1986, Voyager, first unrefueled nonstop flight around the world, 9 days, 3 minutes, 44 seconds

- 1 March to 20 March 1999, Breitling Orbiter 3, first nonstop flight around the world in a balloon; 19 days, 1 hour, 49 minutes

- 19 June to 3 July 2002, Spirit of Freedom, first solo nonstop flight around the world in a balloon; 14 days, 19 hours, 50 minutes

- 17 December 2003, 100th anniversary of first human-controlled and self-propelled flight of an airplane

Appendix II

First Flights at Edwards Air Force Base

First flights are always considered a risky business. Test pilot, astronaut, and manager for the space shuttle orbital test program Donald K. "Deke" Slayton put it very well when he cautioned prior to the first flight of the space shuttle Columbia: "In my opinion, about 90 percent of your risk in a total program comes with a first flight. There is no nice inbetween milestone. You have to bite it all in one chunk." NASA's associate administrator for space transportation systems, John Yardley, explained at the same time: "I'm not worried over any of the problems we have worried about. They're in good shape. The things that you have to be careful about are the unknowns, things that have never happened before. A new engineering gremlin could crawl out of the woodwork, one nobody could have predicted."

Muroc Army Air Base was selected for the maiden flight of the Bell XP-59A Airacomet, America's first jet-powered aircraft, because of the remoteness of its high desert location, the clear and uncrowded skies, and the incalculable measure of safety afforded by the vast expanse of Rogers Dry Lake, which could (and would again and again) serve as an emergency landing field should any inflight problems occur. In the years since, these unsurpassed natural advantages have been augmented by sophisticated range tracking and communications equipment and a corps of technical and emergency response personnel trained to deal with any contingency. All of these resources, when combined, continue to make Edwards the optimum location for the first flights of high-performance and experimental aircraft.

"First flight" is here defined as the first flight of an air vehicle that took off, landed, or both at Edwards Air Force Base. This list represents a conservative compilation of confirmed first flights of new experimental and prototype air vehicles, in addition to subsequent models that encompassed major configuration or system modifications. There is, however, evidence to suggest that at least 20 other types and models of aircraft also completed their first flights at the base.

Key to Acronyms and Abbreviations:

AAW – Active Aeroelastic Wing
ATB – Advanced Technology Bomber
ATF – Advanced Tactical Fighter
AX – Attack, Experimental
CR/W – Canard Rotor/Wing
CRV – Crew Return Vehicle
CTOL – Conventional Takeoff and Landing
CV – (Aircraft) Carrier Version
DFBW – Digital Fly-by-Wire
EAFB – Edwards Air Force Base
FBW – Fly-by-Wire
FSW – Forward-Swept Wing
FX – Fighter, Experimental
JSF – Joint Strike Fighter
LLRV – Lunar Landing Research Vehicle
LWF – Lightweight Fighter
LTV – Ling-Temco-Vought
RPV – Remotely Piloted Vehicle
SCW – Super Critical Wing
SMV – Space Maneuver Vehicle
STOVL – Short Takeoff and Vertical Landing
STS – Space Transportation System
UAV – Unmanned Aerial Vehicle
UCAV – Unmanned Combat Aerial Vehicle
UCAV-N – Unmanned Combat Aerial Vehicle-Navy
V/STOL – Vertical/Short Takeoff and Landing
VTOL – Vertical Takeoff and Landing

The following list of first flights at Edwards Air Force Base gives the date, air vehicle and type, pilot(s), and comments:

— 26 November 1929, Northrop/Avion prototype semiflying wing demonstrator, Eddie Bellande (may have been second flight)
— 2 December 1941, Curtiss-Wright Model CW-29B, J. Harvey Gray, flying subscale mockup for XP-55 Ascender
— 5 December 1941, General Motors Model A-1 "Bug" RPV, unmanned (prototype for a flying jet bomb [JB], i.e., cruise missile)
— 1 October 1942, Bell XP-59A Airacomet, Robert Stanley, America's first turbojet-powered airplane; unofficial first flight (official first flight 2 October 1942; project MX-397)
— 9 January 1943, Lockheed C-69 Constellation, Eddie Allen and Milo Burcham, Burbank to Edwards AFB
— 15 January 1943, Vultee XP-54 Swoose Goose, Frank Davis (project MX-14)
— 18 April 1943, Bell YP-59A Airacomet, Robert Stanley
— 27 August 1943, Northrop JB-1 Bat, Harry Crosby, unpowered jet bomb prototype (project MX-543)
— 6 September 1943, Northrop XP-56 Black Bullet, John Myers (project MX-12)
— 2 October 1943, Northrop Model N-12, Harry Crosby, unpowered concept demonstrator for rocket-powered XP-79 (project MX-334)
— 30 November 1943, Northrop Model N-12, Harry Crosby, unpowered glide flight-powered version of MX-334 (project MX-324)
— 8 January 1944, Lockheed XP-80, Milo Burcham (project MX-409)
— 6 June 1944, Lockheed XP-58 Chain Lightning, Joe Towle, Burbank to Edwards AFB
— 10 June 1944, Lockheed XP-80A, Tony LeVier (two built; second example flew 1 August)
— 7 February 1945, Convair XP-81 Silver Bullet, Frank Davis, prototype composite-powered (piston/jet) fighter
— 12 September 1945, Northrop XP-79B Flying Ram, Harry Crosby, jet-powered version of proposed rocket-powered XP-79 (project MX-365); crashed, killed pilot
— 28 February 1946, Republic XP-84 Thunderjet, Major William Lien
— 17 May 1946, Douglas XB-43, Bob Brush, America's first turbojet-powered bomber (project MX-475)
— 25 June 1946, Northrop XB-35, Max Stanley, prototype semiflying wing bomber (project MX-140)
— 12 September 1946, North American XFJ-1 Fury, Major William Lien, U.S. Navy
— 2 October 1946, Chance Vought XF6U-1 Pirate, Ted Owens, U.S. Navy
— 1 November 1946, Ryan XF2R-1 Dark Shark, Al Conover, composite-powered (piston/jet), U.S. Navy
— 9 November 1946 – Lockheed XR60-1 Constitution, Joe Towle, U.S. Navy, Burbank to Edwards AFB
— 9 December 1946 – Bell X-1, Chalmers

Goodlin, first powered flight
— 17 March 1947, North American XB-45 Tornado, Paul Brewer and George Krebs
— 2 April 1947, Convair XB-46, Ellis Shannon
— 5 April 1947, Hughes XF-11, Howard Hughes, first complete takeoff and safe landing flight
— 15 April 1947, Douglas D-558-1 Skystreak, Gene May, U.S. Navy
— 27 May 1947, Douglas XB-42A, Bob Brush, composite powered (piston/jet) bomber
— 1 October 1947, North American XP-86 Sabre, George Welch
— 21 October 1947, Northrop YB-49, Max Stanley, semiflying wing jet bomber, Hawthorne to Edwards AFB (project MX-51)
— 4 February 1948, Douglas D-558-2 Skyrocket, John Martin, U.S. Navy
— 5 March 1948, Curtiss XP-87 Blackhawk, Lee Miller
— 23 March 1948, Douglas XF3D-1 Skyknight, Russ Thaw, U.S. Navy
— 16 August 1948, Northrop XF-89 Scorpion, Fred Bretcher (project MX-808)
— 23 August 1948, McDonnell XF-85 Goblin, Edwin Schoch, parasite fighter (project MX-472)
— 18 September 1948, Convair XF-92A Dart, Ellis Shannon, delta-wing research (project MX-813)
— 20 October 1948, McDonnell XF-88 Voodoo, Bob Edholm (project MX-812)
— 16 December 1948, Northrop X-4 Bantam, Charles Tucker (project MX-810)
— 16 April 1949, Lockheed YF-94, Tony LeVier, Van Nuys to Edwards AFB
— 9 May 1949, Republic XF-91 Thunderceptor, Carl Bellinger (project MX-809)
— 3 June 1949, Lockheed XF-90, Tony LeVier (project MX-811)
— 22 December 1949, North American YF-86D Sabre Dog, George Welch (formerly designated YF-95A)
— 19 January 1950, Lockheed YF-94C Starfire, Tony LeVier (formerly designated YF-97A)
— 25 January 1950, North American YF-93A Sabre Cat, George Welch
— 4 May 1950, Northrop YRB-49A, Fred Bretcher, semiflying wing reconnaissance bomber
— 26 May 1950, Douglas XA2D-1 Skyshark, George Jansen, turboprop-powered U.S. Navy prototype fighter
— 3 June 1950, Republic YF-84F Thunderstreak, Oscar Haas (formerly designated YF-96A)
— 27 June 1950, Northrop YF-89A Scorpion, John Quinn
— 28 September 1950, Lockheed YF-94B, Tony LeVier
— 22 November 1950, Chance Vought XSSM-N-8 Regulus I, U.S. Navy cruise missile
— 23 January 1951, Douglas XF4D-1 Skyray, Bob Rahn, U.S. Navy
— 20 June 1951, Bell X-5, Jean Ziegler, variable-geometry (swing-wing) demonstrator

— 4 January 1952, North American XA2J-1 Super Savage, C. E. Poage and Robert Taylor, U.S. Navy turboprop-powered version of AJ-1 Savage; Inglewood to Edwards AFB
— 3 February 1952, Republic YRF-84F Thunderflash, Carl Bellinger
— 19 May 1952, Grumman XF10F-1 Jaguar, Corky Meyer, proposed U.S. Navy swing-wing fighter
— 27 June 1952, Bell X-2, Jean Ziegler, unpowered glide flight (first powered flight 18 November 1955
— 20 October 1952, Douglas X-3 Stiletto, Bill Bridgeman, thermodynamic (heat) evaluation
— 28 October 1952, Douglas XA3D-1 Skywarrior, George Jansen, U.S. Navy heavy attack, Long Beach to Edwards AFB
— 14 February, 1953, Bell X-1A, Jean Ziegler, unpowered glide flight (first powered flight 21 February 1953; Jean Ziegler)
— 10 April 1953, North American YF-86H Sabre Jet, Bob Baker
— 25 May 1953, North American YF-100 Super Sabre, George Welch, exceeded Mach 1 in level-attitude flight (first combat-type to do so)
— 14 October 1953, North American X-10 PRV, unmanned
— 24 October 1953, Convair YF-102 Delta Dagger, Dick Johnson
— 5 January 1954, Republic F-84G Thunderjet, George Rudney, first zero-length launch and mat landing (ZELMAL) test
— 4 March 1954, Lockheed XF-104 Starfighter, Tony LeVier (weapon system 303A)
— 7 May 1954, Republic YF-84J Thunderstreak II, Russ Roth
— 16 June 1954, Lockheed XFV-1 Salmon, Herm Salmon, U.S. Navy VTOL demonstrator
— 22 June 1954 – Douglas XA4D-1 Skyhawk, Bob Rahn, U.S. Navy light attack
— 28 June 1954 – Douglas B-66 Destroyer, George Jansen, Long Beach to Edwards AFB
— 23 August 1954 – Lockheed YC-130 Hercules, Stan Betz and Roy Wimmer, Burbank to Edwards AFB
— 29 August 1954, McDonnell F-101A Voodoo, Bob Little
— 20 December 1954, Convair YF-102A Delta Dagger, Dick Johnson, area-ruled version of YF-102
— 25 March 1955, Chance Vought XF8U-1 Crusader, John Konrad, first supersonic U.S. Navy fighter
— 30 June 1955, McDonnell YRF-101A Voodoo, Bob Little
— 22 July 1955, Republic XF-84H Thunderscreech, Henry Beaird, supersonic propeller test bed
— 22 October 1955, Republic YF-105 Thunderchief, Russ Roth
— 31 October 1955, Convair TF-102A Delta Dagger, trainer version of F-102A
— 10 December 1955, Ryan X-13 Vertijet, Pete Girard, jet-powered VTOL demonstrator
— 12 December 1955, Bell X-1E, Joe Walker, unpowered glide flight (first powered flight 15 December 1955)
— 17 February 1956, Lockheed YF-104A

Starfighter, Tony LeVier
— 21 April 1956, Douglas XF5D-1 Skylancer, RAM Ryan, U.S. Navy
— 23 April 1956, Douglas C-133A Cargomaster, J. C. Armstrong, Long Beach to Edwards AFB
— 25 May 1956, Grumman F11F-1F Super Tiger, Corky Meyer, U.S. Navy
— 26 May 1956, Republic YF-105B Thunderchief, Russ Roth
— 29 May 1956, Chance Vought XSSM-N-9 Regulus II cruise missile, U.S. Navy
— 10 September 1956, North American YF-107A Ultra Sabre, Bob Baker
— 26 December 1956, Convair YF-106A Delta Dart, Dick Johnson
— 4 September 1957, Lockheed C-140A JetStar, Burbank to Edwards AFB
— 26 March 1958, North American F-100D Super Sabre, Al Blackburn, first zero-length launch (ZELL) test
— 30 May 1958, Douglas DC-8, A. C. Heimerdinaer, Long Beach to Edwards AFB
— 3 June 1958, Chance Vought XF8U-3 Crusader III (Super Crusader), John Konrad, U.S. Navy
— 10 April 1959, Northrop T-38A Talon, Lew Nelson
— 8 June 1959, North American X-15A, Scott Crossfield, unpowered glide flight (first powered flight 17 September 1959)
— 30 July 1959, Northrop N-156F Freedom Fighter, Lew Nelson, to YF-5A
— 4 November 1959, Lockheed Model CL-475, Vaughn Krug, rigid-rotor test bed
— 24 November 1959, Hiller X-18, George Bright and Bruce Jones, tilt-wing V/STOL
— 25 January 1962, NASA-Dryden Paresev, Milt Thompson, Paraglider Research Vehicle
— 18 April 1963, Northrop X-21A, Jack Wells, boundary-layer control demonstrator
— 27 May 1963, McDonnell YF-110A Spectre, Bob Little (redesignated YF-4C, renamed Phantom II)
— 23 July 1963, Lockheed F-104A Starfighter, zero-length launch (ZELL) test bed
— 31 July 1963, Northrop YF-5A Freedom Fighter, Hank Chouteau, advanced N-156F
— 16 August 1963, NASA-Dryden M2-F1 lifting body, Milt Thompson, unpowered glide type
— 15 May 1964, Ryan XV-5A, Lou Everett, U.S. Army
— 18 May 1964, McDonnell YRF-110A Spectre, Bob Little, redesignated YRF-4C, renamed Phantom II
— 25 June 1964, North American X-15A-2, Bob Rushworth
— 21 September 1964, North American XB-70A Valkyrie, Al White and Colonel Joe Cotton, supersonic transport (SST) test bed; two built (No. 2 flew 17 July 1965)
— 30 October 1964, Bell Lunar Landing Research Vehicle, Joe Walker
— 25 February 1965, Douglas DC-9, George Jansen
— 12 July 1966, Northrop M2-F2 lifting body, Milt Thompson, unpowered glide flight
— 22 December 1966, Northrop HL-10 lifting body, Bruce Peterson, glide flight (first powered flight 13 November 1968)

— 20 August 1967, Lockheed U-2R, Bill Park, Palmdale to Edwards AFB
— 20 November 1968, LTV A-7B Corsair II, first flight with Allison TF41-A-2 engine
— 28 March 1969, Northrop YF-5B-21, John Fritz
— 17 April 1969, Martin Marietta X-24A lifting body, Jerauld Gentry, unpowered glide flight (first powered flight 19 March 1970)
— 12 December 1969, NASA-Dryden Hyper III, unmanned, high-speed lifting body concept demonstration vehicle
— 2 June 1970, Northrop M2-F3 lifting body, Jerauld Gentry, glide flight (first powered flight 25 November 1970)
— 29 August 1970, Douglas DC-10, Clifford Stout, Long Beach to Edwards AFB
— 9 March 1971, NASA F-8A SCW, Tom McMurtry, one built
— 31 August 1971, Martin Marietta YQM-93A Compass Dwell RPV, unmanned
— 25 March 1972, NASA F-8C DFBW, Gary Krier, one built
— 10 May 1972, Republic YA-10A AX demonstrator, Howard Nelson, two built
— 30 May 1972, Northrop YA-9A AX demonstrator, Lew Nelson, two built
— 27 July 1972, McDonnell Douglas F-15 Eagle FX demonstrator, Irving Burrows
— 11 August 1972, Northrop F-5E Tiger II
— 28 July 1973, Boeing YQM-94A Compass Cope B RPV Gull, unmanned
— 1 August 1973, Martin Marietta X-24B lifting body, unmanned, first glide flight (first powered flight 15 November 1973); modified Martin Marietta X-24A
— 2 February 1974, General Dynamics YF-16 LWF demonstrator, Phil Oestricher, two built (second example flew 9 May 1974)
— 9 June 1974, Northrop YF-17 Cobra LWF demonstrator, Hank Chouteau, two built (second example flew 21 August 1974)
— 17 August 1974, Ryan YQM-98A Compass Cope RPV Tern, unmanned
— 25 September 1974, Northrop F-5F, two-seat version of F-5E Tiger II
— 23 December 1974, Rockwell B-1A, Charles Bock and Colonel Ted Sturmthal, four built
— 26 August 1975, McDonnell Douglas YC-15 AMST, Major John Harris and Ken Lewis
— 12 August 1977, Rockwell space shuttle *Enterprise*, first of several unpowered glide flights
— 4 May 1979, Fairchild Republic YA-10B, Thunderbolt II, two-seat night attack version of A-10A, Wendy Shawler
— 27 August 1979, Rockwell HiMAT RPV, unmanned, subscale fighter demonstrator; two built (second example flew)
— 21 December 1979, NASA AD-1 oblique wing concept demonstrator, Tom McMurtry
— 14 April 1981, Rockwell space shuttle *Columbia*, STS-1, Robert Crippen and John Young (first orbital flight; recovered at Edwards AFB)
— 30 August 1982, Northrop F-20A Tigershark, Russ Scott, three built
— 18 October 1984, Rockwell B-1B Lancer, M. L. Evenson and Lieutenant Colonel Leroy Schroeder, Palmdale to Edwards AFB

— 11 December 1984, Grumman X-29 FSW demonstrator, Charles Sewell
— 15 October 1985, Fairchild Republic T-46A, Jamor Martinez
— 2 December 1987, Sikorsky/DARPA/NASA X-Wing, Richard Faull and Warren Hall
— 17 July 1989, Northrop B-2A Spirit ATB, Bruce Hinds and Colonel Richard Couch
— 5 April 1990, Pegasus space booster, unmanned, air-launch
— 27 August 1990, Northrop YF-23 ATF demonstrator, Paul Metz, two built (second example flew 26 October 1990)
— 29 September 1990, Lockheed YF-22 ATF demonstrator, Dave Ferguson, two built (second example flew 30 October 1990)
— 15 September 1991, McDonnell Douglas C-17A Globemaster III, William Casey, and Lieutenant Colonel George London
— 21 December 1993, Aurora Flight Services Perseus A RPV, unmanned
— 29 March 1996, Lockheed RQ-3A DarkStar, unmanned, Tier III Plus UAV
— 24 May 1996, Aurora Flight Services Theseus RPV, unmanned
— 16 December 1996, LoFLYTE, unmanned, subscale model of NASA hypersonic wave-rider vehicle
— 17 May 1997, McDonnell Douglas X-36, unmanned, 28 percent subscale model of tailless fighter
— 28 February 1998, Teledyne Ryan RQ-4A Global Hawk, unmanned, Tier II Plus UAV
— 12 March 1998, Scaled Composites X-38 CRV, unmanned
— August 1998, Boeing X-40A SMV, unmanned
— 10 November 1998, AeroVironment Centurion high-altitude RPV, unmanned
— 6 February 1999, Scaled Composites X-38 CRV, unmanned, unpowered glide flight
— 29 June 1999, Orbital Sciences X-34, unmanned
— 8 September 1999, AeroVironment Helios high-altitude RPV, unmanned
— 18 September 2000, Boeing X-32A JSF demonstrator, Fred Knox, CTOL version
— 24 October 2000, Lockheed Martin X-35A JSF demonstrator, Tom Morgenfeld, CTOL and CV version
— 16 December 2000, Lockheed Martin X-35C JSF demonstrator, Joe Sweeney, CV version
— 14 March 2001, Boeing X-40A SMV, unmanned, unpowered glide flight
— 29 March 2001, Boeing X-32B JSF demonstrator, Dennis O'Donoghue, STOVL version
— 3 July 2001, Lockheed Martin X-35B JSF demonstrator, Simon Hargreaves, STOVL version, Palmdale to Edwards AFB (first full flight; had hovered previously at Palmdale)
— 22 May 2002, Boeing X-45A UCAV demonstrator, unmanned, two built (second example flew 21 November 2002)
— 15 November 2002, Boeing/NASA F/A-18A AAW, Dana Purifoy

(Note: The foregoing was compiled by the Air Force Flight Test Center History Office and the Air Force Flight Test Center Museum.)

Appendix III
Dedicated and Other Types of Research Air Vehicles

(Note: This list is organized by manufacturer and designation, purpose, and comments.)

— Bell X-1, high-speed flight—up to and beyond Mach 1.0, supersonic speed; its design goal was first met 14 October 1947 with a flight to Mach 1.06
— Bell X-2, high-speed flight—up to and beyond Mach 2.0 with sweptback flying surfaces, ultimately reached Mach 3.196
— Douglas X-3 Stiletto, high-temperature (thermal heating) flight test evaluations, did not meet its design goal of speeds between Mach 1.5 to 2.0
— Northrop X-4 Bantam, semitailless subsonic flight test evaluations, met and/or exceeded all of its design goals
— Bell X-5, variable-geometry (swing-wing) flight test evaluations, met and/or exceeded all of its design goals
— Convair X-6 Crusader, nuclear-fueled/powered propulsion system test bed for proposed nuclear-powered bomber (NPB) WS-125A, which was not pursued; full and final test results were never released to the public
— Lockheed X-7, ramjet propulsion system test bed
— Aerobee X-8, high-altitude research rocket
— Bell X-9 Shrike, air-launched rocket
— North American X-10, cruise missile
— Convair X-11, Atlas ICMB test vehicle
— Convair X-12, Atlas ICBM test vehicle
— Ryan X-13 Vertijet, turbojet-powered VTOL evaluations
— Bell X-14, VTOL air vehicle
— North American X-15A, very-high-speed, very-high-altitude demonstrator, speed (Mach 6.0) and altitude (300,000 feet) design goals were met and/or exceeded
— North American X-15A-2, highly modified X-15A—optimized to exceed original design goals, attained maximums of Mach 6.70 and 354,200 feet
— Bell X-16, high-altitude research; not built
— Lockheed X-17, high-altitude research rocket
— Hiller X-18, VTOL rotorcraft
— Curtiss X-19, VTOL converti-plane
— Boeing X-20 Dyna-Soar, proposed orbital reconnaissance vehicle; not proceeded with Northrop X-21A, boundary-layer control test bed
— Bell X-22, V/STOL research aircraft
— Martin-Marietta X-23A, precision recovery including maneuvering entry (PRIME) lifting-body flight test air vehicle
— Martin Marietta X-24A, advanced X-23A
— Martin Marietta X-24B, advanced X-24A
— Martin Marietta X-24C, proposed high-speed demonstrator; not built Lockheed X-24C, proposed high-speed demonstrator; not built Bensen X-25, lightweight helicopter Bensen X-25A, improved lightweight helicopter Bensen X-25B, same as X-25A but with more powerful engine Schweizer X-26 Frigate

— Lockheed X-27 Lancer, highly advanced lightweight fighter demonstrator; not proceeded with Pereira X-28 Osprey Grumman X-29, forward-swept wing and advanced technology demonstrator
— X-30, National Aero Space Plane (NASP); not proceeded with Rockwell/MBB X-31, enhanced fighter maneuverability (EFM) Boeing X-31A Vectoring extremely short takeoffs and landings (ESTOL) control tailless operation research (VECTOR)
— Boeing X-32A, conventional takeoff and landing/aircraft carrier-type (CTOL/CV) joint strike fighter (JSF) demonstrator for U.S. Air Force and U.S. Navy Boeing X-32B, short takeoff and vertical landing (STOVL) JSF demonstrator for U.S. Marine Corps, Royal Navy, and Royal Air Force Lockheed Martin X-33 VentureStar, proposed space shuttle replacement; not proceeded with
— Orbital Sciences X-34 reusable launch vehicle (RLV)
— Lockheed Martin X-35A, conventional takeoff and landing (CTOL) Joint Strike Fighter (JSF) demonstrator for the U.S. Air Force
— Lockheed Martin X-35B, short takeoff and vertical landing (STOVL) JSF demonstrator for U.S. Marine Corps, Royal Navy, and Royal Air Force
— Lockheed Martin X-35C, aircraft carrier-type (CV) JSF demonstrator for U.S. Navy Boeing X-36 tailless fighter agility research aircraft
— Boeing X-37A reusable launch vehicle (RLV)
— Scaled Composites X-38A crew return vehicle (CRV), first flown March 1998; three built; program canceled 29 April 2002
— U.S. Air Force X-39, classified Boeing X-40A space maneuver vehicle (SMV), 90 percent scale model of a proposed SMV; flown once on 11 August 1998—100 miles per hour at 9,000 feet
— U.S. Air Force X-41 common aero vehicle (CAV), suborbital experimental maneuverable reentry vehicle; to test the feasibility of creating a future military space plane (MSP); other details are not available
— U.S. Air Force X-42, pop-up upper stage liquid-fueled booster rocket to deliver 2,000- to 4,000-pound payloads into low Earth orbit (other details are not available)
— Boeing X-43A Hyper-X, air-launched subscale hypersonic scramjet engine testbed; unsuccessful first flight June 2001; test flights were scheduled to resume in mid- to late-2003 and early 2004
— Lockheed Martin X-44A, multiaxis no-tail aircraft (MANTA), based on F/A-22 Raptor; was to fly before 2007 but program was canceled
— Boeing X-45A Shrike, unmanned combat aerial vehicle (UCAV) demonstrator, two built
— Boeing X-45B, larger version of the X-45A to demonstrate the feasibility of an operational UCAV
— Boeing X-46 (no details)
— Northrop Grumman X-47A Pegasus, two built

— Northrop Grumman X-47B Pegasus, larger version of the X-47A to demonstrate the feasibility of an operational UCAV
— NASA-Langley/Boeing X-48A (no details)
— X-49 (classified; no details)
— Boeing X-50A Dragonfly, unmanned canard rotor/wing (CR/W) demonstrator

Other Research Types:
Convair XF-92A, delta-wing test bed
Douglas D-558-1 Skystreak, high-speed research with straight flying surfaces
Douglas D-558-2 Skyrocket, high-speed research with sweptback flying surfaces
NASA AD-1, oblique-wing research
NASA M2-F1, lifting body research
NASA M2-F2, lifting body research
NASA M2-F3, lifting body research
Northrop HL-10, lifting body research
NASA HL-20, personnel launch system (PLS) research lifting body-type air vehicle; full-scale mockup only; precursor of the X-38 CRV (which see above)
North American XB-70A Valkyrie, supersonic transport (SST) flight test research, Mach 3.08 and 74,000 feet attained
Vought XC-142A, tilt-rotor research

INDEX